Render unto Caesar

An exploration of faith and politics

Nathan Driscoll

PUBLISHING

First published 2022 by Malcolm Down Publishing Ltd.
www.malcolmdown.co.uk

24 23 22 22 7 6 5 4 3 2 1

The right of Nathan Driscoll to be identified as the author of this work has been asserted by him in accordance with the Copyright, Designs and Patents Act 1988.

British Library Cataloguing in Publication Data
A catalogue record for this book is available from the British Library.

ISBN 978-1-915046-09-3

Cover design by Esther Kotecha
Art direction by Sarah Grace

Printed in the UK

Contents

Acknowledgements

I want to thank my wife for her unfailing support and encouragement. She has read through many drafts, always giving me helpful advice and guidance. Without her as a sounding board I would be under the delusion that everything I write is crystal clear!

I want to thank my friend Tim Edwards for his support and the ideas he gives me through our conversations, as well as his meticulous checking of the script. Both my wife and Tim have helped me see the places where the argument has needed amendment. I also want to thank my friend Philip Ware for his ever-present encouragement and support. Conversations with three other Christian friends about politics, the Old Testament and other contemporary issues have also been invaluable.

When I started researching this book I read *On Politics* by Alan Ryan; it gave me a really good basis from which to begin thinking through the issues. His fluent, discursive style with occasional flashes of humour has really helped.

Once again, I am very grateful to my publisher, Malcolm Down, who has given me the opportunity to reflect on this ever-topical subject, as well as Sheila Jacobs for her detailed and perceptive editorial guidance. I also want to thank Sarah Grace for her excellent artwork for both *The Good Question* and for this book. I also want to thank Esther Kotecha for her striking contributions.

Preface

I have written this book because I wanted to question what the Christian faith has to say about politics – I want you to read it asking yourself the same question. In fact, I hope you will ask yourself a series of questions, such as this one:

Q. Should the Church stay out of politics?

You can see straightaway that not everyone will have the same view. Some will say the Church should stay out of politics *unless* it directly affects the practice of faith; others will say that the Church is there to show compassion but should never directly align itself with a particular political party, and still others claim that the Church, in line with biblical injunctions against poverty, should fight for 'social justice' by getting its hands 'dirty' through involvement in political campaigns. There is also a much publicised part of the Church that seeks to affect attitudes towards sexual morality through political action.[1]

I cannot tell you what combination of these views to adopt but I am sure you can identify your own sensibilities. Once you have done that, you will have an anchor point from which you can assess the various ideas that come at you. Some of those ideas will come, later on in the book, from political philosophers: I will try to make their ideas as accessible as possible. Why do we need to listen to such ideas? It is because in some measure or other they have influenced the way we are governed now. They will provide a context for us to think about our faith and its connection with political life.

---

1. For example see, Jessica Glenzer, "'It shakes you to your core": the anti-abortion extremists gaining ground on the right', 6 July 2021, www.theguardian.com/us-news/2021/jul/06/anti-abortion-activists-operation-save-america (accessed 20 October 2021).

I watch the BBC Six O'Clock News on most days. The top stories regularly cover the health service, refugees, the pandemic, climate change, food banks, education, discrimination or crime. Most, if not all, of the problems are beyond my reach and I watch with a combination of curiosity, concern and resignation. On Sundays at church we pray for our leaders, particular trouble spots in the world, for the sick, for those who serve us in the community and for persecuted Christians across the world.

I usually avoid talking to people about politics, especially at church, unless I happen to know that their views coincide with mine. I certainly don't want to offend anyone and in any event, I enjoy worshipping and learning together and do not want to detract from it. Topics to be avoided include Brexit, sexuality and which political party I voted for. That approach has the advantage of avoiding needless confrontation, but it does leave a few gaps. I do, like many, have strong feelings about what goes on in the world and writing this book has helped me articulate them.

Q. What are the political questions that worry you the most?

I wanted to discover how Christians have thought about faith and politics over time and so the first chapter is partly historical. If you are familiar with the history of the Church, you may want to ask yourself if your version concurs with mine. As I researched the history I also realised that lives must be very different under different types of authority. Those different forms of government include democracy, like ours in Great Britain, totalitarianism, such as found in North Korea or China, and theocracy, as practised in Iran or Saudi Arabia. Has Christianity anything to say about *the way* people are governed? Is there such a thing as a Christian state, and if there is, how would unbelievers be treated? What are the risks in allowing people freedom, and what are the deficits in taking it away from them? How costly is it to challenge injustice when you live under a corrupt regime? When the ultimate loyalty demanded of citizens is towards the state, can minorities practise their faith without fear? Do countries which are run by small groups of religious leaders represent God, or do those leaders just use religious 'authority' to represent themselves? These are some of the questions I try to address knowing that it is much easier to be morally confident in theory than in practice.

We live in a world where governments, investors and companies play an enormous game of 'chess' for resources, trading routes and an increased share of the global 'marketplace'. State boundaries and régime types are no longer relevant when it comes to investment decisions. Alliances between nations are based on economic advantage, military threat and sometimes religious and national identities. Those alliances can easily shift, so special relationships are not always that special. In among this matrix, where do the notions of justice, honesty and compassion fit in? Do they mean anything in the higher reaches of diplomacy, or is the standard technique always to point out the mutual benefit of a policy to the other side? Where is the place for the well-being of the poor? Do protests about human rights abuses really cut any ice in a world where national interests appear to take precedence?

The key question this book poses

Does Christ's ministry, death and resurrection help us when it comes to our participation in and understanding of political life? This book represents a journey in my reading, thinking and discussions with others about what faith can bring to the way we are governed, and our part in it. I hope it will help you in your own reflections and conversations with others.

Introduction

The book of Genesis is principally about the start of God's relationship with humanity. After the Fall and the Flood, God 'regretted that he had made human beings on the earth, and his heart was deeply troubled' because of the extent of human wickedness.[2] Consequently, the Law was given. In addition to the moral and spiritual force of the Ten Commandments, the practical instructions for living in Exodus and Leviticus were detailed and prescriptive, constituting a radical set of rules for an explicitly primitive and idolatrous society, a society with which we have no cultural empathy. The Old Testament goes on to describe a series of political arrangements involving judges, kings and relations between Israel and other nations. God's aim of keeping His chosen people holy was in the end a story of human failure and bloodshed interspersed by shafts of moral regeneration delivered by the prophets and a few righteous leaders.

It is sometimes claimed that it is God who has failed because human beings have rejected Him. My approach to this problem is that it is *not* a failure for God to have opened Himself to rejection, but it *would* be a failure had He not been able to accept and overcome it. For me, the death and resurrection of Christ is clear evidence that God, in human form, has done just that. Some Christians are uncomfortable with the idea that God's sovereignty might be jeopardised through Him releasing absolute control, preferring to focus on the idea of God's foreknowledge of history. I find it easier to relate to the former idea of God opening Himself to uncertainty as it concurs with my own understanding of what is entailed in a trusting relationship.

---

2. Genesis 6:6.

Q. In human relationships, if we cannot open ourselves to rejection, does it also mean that we cannot genuinely receive affection?

The hope of the Messiah was embedded in the Old Testament, but Emmanuel, when He came, did not bring about a political revolution or a military campaign, let alone a structure for governing society.[3] During Christ's time on earth, the Roman Empire occupied Jewish 'Palestine'[4] but Christ made no attempt to overthrow the regime; He was more concerned about the synagogue leaders' hypocrisy. All in all, the Bible is *not* a manual of procedures as to how to run a country.

While offering no advice about what form of political authority should prevail, Christ was the catalyst for two covert revolutionary ideas. Firstly, He overturned the idea of God's *kingdom* being about territory to one of renewed mind, heart and spirit; the kingdom was no longer a promised land but rather an inner spiritual rebirth.[5] Equally radical was Christ's insistence that *all* are worthy of God's mercy and compassion; God's promises were no longer to be seen as given for the Jewish people alone.

The Pharisees and Sadducees were convinced that *only* they were accepted by God; St Paul points out that they had wrongly come to this conclusion when he wrote that *all* were sons of God regardless of whether they were *Jew or Greek*.[6] The Jewish leaders of the time were also ignoring significant elements of their own Scriptures. In Isaiah 49:6

---

3. The names, Messiah, Emmanuel and Christ are used interchangeably to mean 'God the Son', that is, God in human form. I will use 'Christ' from here onwards.

4. This included Idumaea, Judea, Galilee and Samaria.

5. Over many centuries the Israelites had ignored the connection between God's love and mercy, the Law and the prospect of the Promised Land; the latter, the Promised Land, was irrevocably intertwined with former, that is, obeying the Law and enjoying God's grace and mercy. See Gordon & Stephen Kuhrt, *Believing in Baptism: Understanding and Living God's Covenant Sign* (London: T&T Clark, 2020), Chapter 3.

6. Galatians 3:28.

the Lord says, 'I will also make you a light for the Gentiles, that my salvation may reach to the ends of the earth.' In Psalm 22:27, the psalm which echoed the story of the crucifixion, we read that 'all the families of the nations will bow down before him'. The Pharisees and Sadducees had wrongly concluded that they were a divine elite rather than a conduit for God to reach out to all.

Q. How would you describe the difference between Christ's interpretations of the Scriptures compared to the Jewish people of His time?

By the end of the first millennium, powers from the Mediterranean, Asia and the Middle East clashed in prolonged conflicts; territories were constantly disputed and ordinary people often lived in perpetual fear for their lives. The rules of war were merciless, and more often than not accompanied by gruesome and gratuitous violence. Religious affirmation, the search for human and material resources, the drive for political power and self-aggrandisement were among the chief motives for empire building. Had Christ's revolutionary ideas come to be reinterpreted to mean the exact opposite of what was originally intended?

The Crusades were attempts by Western monarchs and the papacy to reclaim the Holy Land for pilgrimage, political control and affirmation of God's approval by means of eradicating and expelling Islamic peoples and their governments. By the late Middle Ages in Europe, ethnic and religious 'cleansing' had become part and parcel of political life. The Jews were almost always the first to fall victim to such atrocities.

After the Reformation in the sixteenth century, when the chains between Church and state loosened, an opening slowly emerged towards modern and more familiar forms of government. From the sixteenth century onwards, industrialisation, colonial trading and the expansion of forced labour and slavery changed the face of both the Western and New Worlds; a new economic opportunity for investors, traders, nobles and monarchs was mixed in with traditional religious fervor. Monarchs and a small group of aristocrats together with the Church were no longer up to the task of governing increasingly complex societies. In the first part of the twentieth century, the scope of universal suffrage had widened to include the majority of adult citizens, including women; governments in Britain could be unseated by the electorate. Once the votes are cast, the battle for the mind of the voter is still fought out between the political elites, with business and the media influencing the outcomes.

Since 1945, Western Europe has enjoyed an unprecedented period of relative peace, but much else has been happening in other less visible parts of the world. According to the Economic Intelligence Unit's 2020 Democracy Index, approximately only a half of the world's people currently live in a democracy.[7] That means that as the global population approaches 8 billion in 2021 almost *4 billion* people live under explicitly authoritarian regimes or other arrangements which are *not* democratic.[8] The notion that 'progress' is unrelenting over time is in serious doubt. Understandably, when we listen to the news we hear the most about our own country; we should remember that the many places we do not receive news from is because of the censorship imposed by authoritarian governments, or because it contains no strategic interest for audiences. We hear about the state of democracy a great deal, but much less about theocracy, totalitarianism and fragile governments where corruption dominates life. For example, whereas we expect all murders to be

---

7. Please see:
https://byjus.com/free-ias-prep/democracy-index-eiu/#:~:text=Economic%20 Intelligence%20Unit%20%28EIU%29%20has%20released%20the%20 13th,COVID-19%20on%20democracy%20and%20freedom%20across%20the%20 world (accessed 15 June 2021).

8. These are known as hybrid states under the Economic Intelligence Unit's Democracy Index.

recorded and reported, there are many places where this is not the case. The world has changed since I grew up in the 1950s. In post-war Britain economic recovery, the Cold War between the US and the USSR (Russia, as it is now), the miners' strike, the conflict in Northern Ireland and becoming part of the European Union are some of the things that stand out in my memory. Today the nation state has become more protective of its borders, given the number of displaced people and refugees in the world, while the trade boundaries and networks can cross continents at the touch of an investor's computer click. The West no longer dominates the global economy, with mid-Asia and the Far East increasingly influencing trade. Africa lags behind economically, but richer economies and companies are purloining the natural resources there. The oil-rich theocracies complicate the already deep tribal and religious conflicts in the Middle East and the media have a much tighter grip on what we know and what we don't know. The new colonialism is economic and modern slavery is predicated on the plight of desperate, trapped and vulnerable people. Human rights abuses are spread across the globe. In the middle of all this are huge issues around climate change; there is a tension between developing new technologies and curbing our consumerist appetites.

Against this backdrop, to focus only on the issues between Conservatives or Labour supporters (in the UK) and Republicans or Democrats (in the US) does not answer the problems of the disenfranchised; they have no effective political choice, no right of free expression and no hope of being treated fairly under the law. To steer a pathway out of poverty in a modern liberal democracy is hard enough, but in a totalitarian regime it is virtually impossible. Therefore, any approach to politics must to some extent depend upon the type of government we find ourselves living under; for if we live under an autocratic regime, our priorities are much more likely to centre on basic rights of freedom, whereas in a modern liberal democracy, our interests will more likely concern economic opportunity, education, health, discrimination and the gap between public and private life.

Q. Should we concern ourselves about the way other countries govern, or do we have enough to worry about in our own backyard?

So where does that leave us when it comes to the relevance of faith to political life? Christ focused on principles rather than policies; He did not come to negotiate trade deals, develop devolved government, decide on levels of income tax or even overthrow regimes, but to help everyone look at their motives and true aspirations, rulers included. In that way His teachings about morality and faith apply not only to all aspects of living, but to every humanly constructed institution as well.

The purpose of this book is to examine how the Christian faith is relevant to the political problems of modern societies. When is it right to acquiesce and when is it right to resist? St Paul's letter to the Romans has been interpreted in more than one way; some have said that authorities must be obeyed no matter what, while others say that they are there for our good and so can be challenged.[9] Does God allow rulers to operate to

---

9. See Romans 13:1-7: 'Let everyone be subject to the governing authorities, for there is no authority except that which God has established. The authorities that exist have been established by God. Consequently, whoever rebels against the authority is rebelling against what God has instituted, and those who do so will bring judgment on themselves. For rulers hold no terror for those who do right, but for those who do wrong. Do you want to be free from fear of the one in authority? Then do what is right and you will be commended. For the one in authority is God's servant for your good. But if you do wrong, be afraid, for rulers do not bear the sword for no reason. They are God's servants, agents of wrath to bring punishment on the wrongdoer. Therefore, it is necessary to submit to the authorities, not only because of possible punishment but also as a matter of conscience. This is also why you pay taxes, for the authorities are God's servants, who give their full time to governing. Give to everyone what you owe them: If you owe taxes, pay taxes; if revenue, then revenue; if respect, then respect; if honour, then honour.'

a different set of moral precepts than the rest of us?[10] Are Christians just there to patch things up? What about sexual morality, gender politics and sanctity of life issues? How involved in politics should Christians be, and how should they conduct themselves?[11] Does politics inform faith, or does faith inform politics, or are the two completely separate?

St Augustine's *City of God*[12] was, and still is, a seminal work which examines the difference between heavenly justice and earthly reality.[13] Will that distinction help us understand something about the relative significance of faith and politics? The first chapter deals with this question through the lens of Church history.

---

10. See Mark 7:5-8: 'So the Pharisees and teachers of the law asked Jesus, "Why don't your disciples live according to the tradition of the elders instead of eating their food with defiled hands?" He replied, "Isaiah was right when he prophesied about you hypocrites; as it is written: "'These people honour me with their lips, but their hearts are far from me. They worship me in vain; their teachings are merely human rules.' You have let go of the commands of God and are holding on to human traditions."'

11. See Haroon Siddique, 'Archbishop of Canterbury, I am not too political, Justin Welby defends his comments on inequality and backs UN report on UK poverty', 2 December 2018, www.theguardian.com/uk-news/2018/dec/02/archbishop-of-canterbury-i-am-not-too-political-justin-welby (accessed 20 October 2021).

12. St Augustine, *City of God* (trans. Henry Bettenson, 1972; London: Penguin Classics, 2003, first published 1467).

13. See Matthew 6:19-21: 'Do not store up for yourselves treasures on earth, where moths and vermin destroy, and where thieves break in and steal. But store up for yourselves treasures in heaven, where moths and vermin do not destroy, and where thieves do not break in and steal. For where your treasure is, there your heart will be also.'

Chapter One: Two Kingdoms

There is a series on television called *Who Do You Think You Are?*[14] In each programme, research teams look into the family histories of a chosen celebrity; like all of us, the celebrities are fascinated to learn about their forebears, and are often surprised to find out how generations before them had to cope with the trials and tribulations of life. They often feel a close connection to them.

Why, then, do so many Christians feel disconnected from Church history? We talk about the 'church family' but the further back we go, the more distant the reality becomes. What was it like to be a Christian in AD800? How was the Church structured? Could everyone read? How powerful was the Church in everyday life for ordinary people? It is difficult to compare the life of a feudal serf to ours in the twenty-first century. Sometimes, it can all feel like a hazy mist, and the concrete lives of the apostles are easier to grasp for no other reason than that we study the Bible week by week. We want to 'grow' in our faith, and Church history might seem irrelevant.

I believe it is important to know where Christians have made mistakes, where they have excelled, where they have failed to make an impact and where their faith has shone out brightly against all the odds. In each generation there are most likely examples of all of these variants, so a generalised history will always miss out nuances, details and exceptions to the rule. This chapter is an attempt to provide a sweep over two millennia since Christ was on earth; it can only touch the most general of trends, but hopefully it will provide an impression. Central to this chapter is the matter of how closely the Church is allied to the state;

---

14. BBC; distributor: Warner Bros Television Productions UK.

one thing is certain – namely, that the relationship between the two has dramatically changed over time. We need to know the history of Church and state if we are to assess how best the relationship should work today.

The City of God

Imagine being a Christian convert living in the second half of the first century, thirty or so years after the death and resurrection of Christ. Your family is Jewish and has disowned you for going against rabbinical traditions handed down over thousands of years. They say only the Jews can know God; Christ said God's love is for everyone and you are convinced it is. The New Testament does not exist yet, and some of your fellow Christians are uncertain as to how to share their faith with people like the Greeks in Ephesus. What you do know has been handed down through the apostles and through letters and documents which circulate between Christian churches. Some groups of Christians, like the one you belong to, are tolerated by the authorities, while others are persecuted and imprisoned because they threaten the social order by their refusal to worship the Roman pagan gods. The orthodox Jewish communities have an obvious vested interest in joining forces with the Roman authorities because this new religion takes away some of their own people.

New Christians are taught to obey the civic authorities; those authorities have been given their power by God in order to promote good. But even if the authorities act out of pure self interest and treat minorities like yours with contempt, cruelty and violence, you are to suffer without rebelling while refusing to give up your faith. To start a conflict with the authorities would compromise its purity and authenticity.

Many early Christians were expecting Christ to return immanently and died not knowing what the future would hold.

The numbers of Christians grew as the first and second centuries unfolded. They were persecuted or tolerated depending on where they lived and whether the incumbent Roman emperor favoured Christians. There were competing gods in the Roman Empire, but early in the fourth century the emperor Constantine thought he saw a message from the God of the Christians in the sun, which he was in the habit of worshipping. He went on with his army to capture Rome and attributed the victory to the Christian God; by the end of the fourth century, Christianity had become the official religion of the Roman Empire.

Q. The disciples were filled with the Holy Spirit and went out to preach the gospel to the world (see Acts 2). Constantine saw a vision which he believed was a message from God which would help him gain a military victory. Which of the two experiences are consistent with Christ's teaching – the disciples' or Constantine's?

The change from being a minority sect to an official state religion had come about not through an inner change of heart but a vision connected to military conquest.[15] As this transition took place, a man called Augustine of Hippo wrote a book called the *City of God*. By the time Augustine was writing he was quoting the New Testament as well as the Old as part of the inspired Word of God. The four Gospels were most likely completed by the end of the first century.[16] Two of the Gospel writers, Matthew and John, were eyewitnesses and two others had close associations with key figures; Mark is said to have gained a great deal of information from the apostle Peter,[17] and Luke was closely associated with the church at Antioch, meeting many closely connected with the

---

15. Bamber Gascoigne, *A Brief History of Christianity* (London: Robinson, 2003), pp. 16-17.

16. Frederick Fyvie Bruce, *The New Testament Documents: Are They Reliable?* (San Francisco, CA: Bottom of the Hill Publishing, 2013), p. 14.

17. Op. cit. p. 32.

gospel story.[18] There was little doubt among the early Christians that these were genuine accounts. There was more uncertainty initially about a few of the shorter letters, namely Hebrews, 2 Peter, 2 and 3 John, James and Jude and the book of Revelation. Ecclesiastical councils in Hippo Regis (393) and Carthage (397) eventually confirmed their inclusion in the New Testament cannon. The Gospels, Acts, and the longer letters by Paul had been accepted as inspired scripture by Christians from the outset.[19]

In the *City of God* and his many other writings, Augustine described what he believed to be the whole story from *God's perspective*. Human governments are there because of the Fall, namely, Adam's sin; otherwise, he thought, there would be no wrongdoing and no *need* for political authority. The hope of the Second Coming was still fresh in the minds and hearts of Christians, and with it the hope of an immediate pathway to the City of God. This is a city where God's elect are in perfect harmony with each other and where there is unblemished justice. Consequently, there can be no perfect government on earth, even though God has allowed human authorities to rule. Augustine believed that God had allowed such rulers to exercise punishments over people; even if those punishments were unjust, Christians had a duty to obey unless they were asked to deny their faith.[20]

St Augustine, by implication, gave human authorities a divine tacit acceptance that they could act justly or unjustly using the earthly

18. Op. cit. p. 37.

19. Op. cit. Chapter 111, pp. 21-26.

20. St Augustine puts it like this: 'While this Heavenly City ... is on pilgrimage in this world, she calls out citizens from all nations ... she takes no account of any difference in customs, laws and institutions, by which earthly peace is achieved and preserved – not that she annuls or abolishes any of those, rather, she maintains them and follows them (for whatever divergences there are among the diverse nations, those institutions have one single aim – earthly peace), provided that no hindrance is presented thereby to the religion which teaches that the one supreme and true God is to be worshipped.' See *City of God, Book XIX*, Chapter 17, p. 878.

standards at their disposal, provided they claimed to be pursuing earthly peace. God would use both evil and good for His purposes, some of which would be unfathomable. Ultimate justice would only be experienced in heaven and in the end, God would choose who would be with Him in heaven. God would in some way include our own choices, but at the same time be above them. Even with the state being officially Christian, we could have no certainty about who might be in God's elect and who might not.

While in a minority, the eyes of Christians could be fixed on the *City of God*, but once Christianity became the state religion of the Roman Empire, the emperor was free to award himself the mantle of 'divine approval' regardless of how he treated people.[21] In conceding that God 'ordains' whoever is in authority, Christians found themselves in a position where they were exhorted to *love their enemies*[22] in church but to *kill them* if they were ordered to by the authorities. To put it another way, if a Christian was ordered to do something which they believed to be morally wrong by the authorities, they were obliged to obey because it was said that God had instituted the ruler; their obedience in carrying out an immoral order, say to kill an innocent person, would contradict the moral force of Christ's teaching. We cannot love our neighbours as ourselves[23] if our 'divinely appointed' ruler orders us to kill them for no good reason.

The next section discusses how the transition from spiritual renewal to territorial conquest played out in subsequent years.

---

21. The emperor Constantine wanted to be remembered as the thirteenth apostle. In 380 Emperor Theodosius described himself as 'the visible God'. See Gascoigne, *A Brief History of Christianity*, p. 21.

22. See Matthew 5:44.

23. See Matthew 19:19.

Holy orders to kill

By the end of the first millennium Christian leaders were not following the example of St Peter in submitting to 'every human authority'.[24] The problem of preserving the faith had grown out of all recognition from its beginnings as a beleaguered minority holding out against attack, torture and exclusion. If God had established *every* authority, why were the authorities fighting each other so readily? One reason was that each authority believed *they* were God's choice so the others must be fraudulent. Another was that faith was no longer a matter of spiritual renewal but rather of political dominance. European states relied on the Church for its ideological influence and the Church relied on kings for their military and policing powers. God had organised a 'tournament between heaven and hell'.[25] Battles, and there were many, would not be won by subservience but by putting the enemies of Christ to the sword. God would show His authority by might, so if a battle was won you were in the right, but if lost, then God would be showing His displeasure at heresy.[26]

What was being fought over? The prizes were the Holy Land, the relics of the gospel story, the sacred places where Jesus had trod and the Temple sites in Jerusalem, which were all places of pilgrimage. The Muslim world also laid claim to Jerusalem from where Mohammed was said to have been taken into heaven and returned to earth during his

---

24. 1 Peter 2:13.

25. This was the basis of a song used to recruit soldiers in support of Louis VII's crusade to revenge the taking of Edessa in 1144 by Zengi, a Muslim leader. This battle for territory symbolised the conflict between Christendom and the Muslim world. See Dan Jones, *The Templars: The Rise and Fall of God's Holy Warriors* (London: Head of Zeus, 2017), Chapter 5.

26. Tom Holland, *Dominion: The Making of the Western Mind*, (London: Little, Brown Book Group, 2019), p. 244. Pope Innocent maintained that God was angry and therefore would not allow Jerusalem to be reclaimed 'while heresy festered'.

life.[27] Possession was equivalent to divine sovereignty and humility had become a sign of betrayal.

The Knights of the Templars were an order of single men who, originally at least, lived as monks but also fought as warriors. They emerged after the First Crusade and occupied castles all over Europe and in the Holy Land, the ultimate prize. The combination of self-denial as an act of worship and developing military expertise and rigorous discipline on the battlefield was seen as the ideal blend of heavenly vision and earthly strength. They would rather die than be taken prisoner. The mix of spirituality with murderous intent is desperately hard to unravel once it buries itself into the warrior-priest's psychology.

It is not hard to see similarities between the Knights of the Templars and twenty-first century religious terrorist organisations. The similarity is not only in the blended cocktail of cruelty and spirituality, but also the infrastructure needed to plan for attack. The Templars diversified into 'banking, estate management and international diplomacy'.[28] In the modern global world money laundering, identity fraud, arranging transport for terrorists, supplying arms, cyber attacks and brainwashing techniques are all equivalents.[29] The First Crusade began at the end of the eleventh century and the Sixth Crusade finally ended with a tenuous negotiated settlement by Frederick II in the middle of the thirteenth century.

Q. What should we say to those who point out the atrocities carried out in the name of Christianity during the Crusades?

---

27. See:
https://bible-quran.com/lailat-al-miraj-muhammad-ascension-heaven/ (accessed 1 September 2021).

28. Jones, *The Templars: The Rise and Fall of God's Holy Warriors*, p. 233.

29. Please see 'Financing of Terrorism: Council of Europe' at www.coe.int/en/web/moneyval/implementation/financing-terrorism (accessed 14 July 2021).

Church and state slowly separate

From the fourteenth century onwards there were no more concerted attempts by Church and state alliances to retake the Holy Land for Christendom. There appears to be no single reason, but the following factors must have had some bearing on why conquering the land where Christ had trod was no longer a realistic ambition. The Plague, the opening up of trading routes to the east, colonisation by European powers in Asia and Africa, the impact of modern printing and the birth of the Protestant Church were all significant changes leading to a different world ahead.

This is not to say that tolerance had arrived in any meaningful way across Europe. Religious purity was still on the agenda but allied to nationalism. For example, on the 30 March 1492, King Ferdinand and Queen Isabella issued an ultimatum to all Jews in Spain, around 200,000, to leave or convert to Christianity.[30] Ferdinand and Isabella's forces also expelled Muslims from Spain in subsequent years. Columbus wrote back saying that his discovery of the New World, the Americas, would provide the wealth to 'rebuild the Temple in Jerusalem'.[31] Ferdinand and Isabella did not take up the invitation.

In 1517 on the eve of All Saints' Day, Martin Luther is reputed to have nailed his ninety-five theses to the church door in Wittenberg, decrying the practice of buying forgiveness from Catholic priests and proclaiming that salvation is through faith alone. He was the founder of the Protestant Church as we know it today. The Protestant Reformation in the early part of the sixteenth century brought about a series of religious conflicts between Catholics and Protestants in France, Germany and the

30. 'Ferdinand and Isabella order expulsion of Jews from Spain', Oxford University Press, Academic insights for the Thinking World. See https://blog.oup.com/2012/03/ferdinand-isabella-order-expulsion-jews-spain/(accessed 14 July 2021) and Gascoigne, *A Brief History of Christianity,* p. 85.

31. Holland, *Dominion: The Making of the Western Mind,* p. 288.

Netherlands.[32] What began to emerge across Europe was that monarchs had to give their allegiance to one side or another, whether willingly or reluctantly. Those who tried to engineer compromises, like Charles IX and Henry III in France, did not succeed. From 1509 to 1702, nine monarchs reigned in England as well as Oliver Cromwell, the anti-monarchist head of state: six were Protestant and four were Catholic. The historic continuity of Catholic dominance had been broken but there was as yet no history of the Protestant Church being *universally* adopted as a state religion.

However, the Protestant Church often followed Catholic tradition with its own determination of heretical belief and where possible, state supported chastisement.[33] Martin Luther's approach to the ruling authorities was based on Romans 13:1: 'Let everyone be subject to the governing authorities, for there is no authority except that which God has established.' On the face of it, Luther was not asking Christians to change their attitude towards authority with the exception of rejecting the dictates and rituals of the Catholic Church. The Papacy and the priesthood were no longer required to be intermediaries between Christians and God. The issue of submitting to ruling authority, showing only passive disobedience when asked to deny one's faith, was reminiscent of the early Christians and Augustine. Then it was a new faith but now it was an old faith with a new 'branch'.

When Christ had talked to the disciples about selling their cloak for a sword in order to fulfil prophecy it would have been easy to interpret that as a call to arms.[34] The meaning of that text appears to be ambiguous but the martyrdoms of Christians in the first and second centuries confirm without doubt that Jesus wanted His message spread by a change of heart

32. Alec Ryrie, *Protestants: The Radicals Who Made the Modern World* (London: William Collins, 2017), pp. 91-95.

33. Op. cit. p. 34.

34. See Luke 22:35-38.

and *not* the take up of arms. The Reformation, as noted above, did not take place without bloodshed. Nevertheless, as the Church splintered in the sixteenth and seventeenth centuries, the original instruction to submit to secular authority was reinstated.

Q. Do we need to ask if a close alliance with the state compromises the Church's independence?

One rule for them and another for us?

Jacques-Bénigne Bossuet was born in 1627, 110 years after Martin Luther's ninety-five theses were made public. He was a devotee of Louis XIV and spent the last four years of his life from 1700-1704 writing *Politics Drawn from Holy Scripture*. After he died, his nephew Abbé Bossuet completed the conclusion using extracts from Augustine's *City of God*. Bossuet was a Catholic theologian who sought to justify again what is popularly known as the 'Divine Right of Kings' where God appoints *both* just and unjust rulers. Through the just rulers He directly orchestrates His purposes, while through the unjust, he allows the purity of the Christian faith to shine out as believers are punished for refusing to deny their trust in God. Bossuet took Christ's passion as the prime example of such acquiescence.

Bossuet believed that absolute rule, through monarchy, is God's ideal because 'Pilate's feebleness', where he succumbed to political expediency allowing Christ to be crucified, demonstrates the grievous alternative.[35] He went as far as to say that Christ acknowledged that Pilate's authority had been conferred on him by God, even as He was being questioned by him before going to the cross.[36] Bossuet maintained that regardless of the

---

35. Jacques-Bénigne Bossuet, Patrick Riley, ed., *Politics Drawn From Holy Scripture*, Cambridge Texts in the History of Political Thought (Cambridge: Cambridge University Press, 1990), Introduction, p. xlviii.

36. Op. cit. lii.

depths of a ruler's abuse of power 'nothing can justify active resistance to his sovereignty –save a king's directly ordaining the violation of divine law, and even then one must passively accept punishment for having passively resisted'.[37]

It was normal for Christ to speak out against injustice during His ministry and He often had to leave places because he knew he might be apprehended by the authorities. For example, when in Jerusalem at an earlier stage of His ministry some Pharisees came to Jesus telling Him to leave as Herod wanted to kill Him. [38] This was not passive resistance. The exception was that He did not attempt to mount a challenge during His trial and crucifixion, having often pointed out He had come to 'give his life as a ransom for many'[39] in line with Old Testament prophecy.

In order to accept Bossuet's interpretation, one has to accept that God the Father intentionally established the authority structure through which His Son would be effectively murdered. Would a parent establish a system through which their own son would be killed for an unjust reason? From a human point of view it is unconscionable to contemplate such an act of treachery, and yet Bossuet proposes that God the Father would contrive the situation in just that way. The core of the Christian faith is that Christ demonstrated God's love for the world through taking the burden of everything that is destructive, even death, upon Himself. St Paul puts it like this:

Christ Jesus:
who, being in very nature God,
did not consider equality with God something to be used to his
own advantage;
rather, he made himself nothing

---

37. Op. cit. li.
38. Luke 13:31.
39. Mark 10:45.

by taking the very nature of a servant,
being made in human likeness.
And being found in appearance as a man,
he humbled himself by becoming obedient to death –
even death on a cross!
Therefore God exalted him to the highest place
and gave him the name that is above every name,
that at the name of Jesus every knee should bow,
in heaven and on earth and under the earth,
and every tongue acknowledge that Jesus Christ is Lord,
to the glory of God the Father.[40]

If Christ's death and resurrection was God sacrificing *Himself* to take on the suffering and sin of the world, it could not *simultaneously* be a means of justifying divine approval for any regime, corrupt, cruel or otherwise. For that to be the case God's character would have to be duplicitous, and whatever else Christ may or may not have thought, it is clear that He considered His Father to be perfect.[41] When Christ said, '… seek first his kingdom and his righteousness … ',[42] He did not add the rider that rulers would be exempt by reason of divine privilege. There are no such exemptions when St Paul discusses judgement.

> You, therefore, have no excuse, you who pass judgment on someone else, for at whatever point you judge another, you are condemning yourself, because you who pass judgment do the same things. Now we know that God's judgment against those who do such things is based on truth. So when you, a mere human being, pass judgment on them and yet do the same

40. Philippians 2:5-11.
41. Matthew 5:48.
42. Matthew 6:33.

things, do you think you will escape God's judgment? Or do you show contempt for the riches of his kindness, forbearance and patience, not realising that God's kindness is intended to lead you to repentance?[43]

Rulers are asked to judge their subjects: the Christian imperative is that they should not impose punishments for acts which they themselves are committing. The parable of the Unmerciful Servant makes this abundantly clear.[44] For God to accept evil acts from rulers but reject them from subjects would mean that righteousness is not at the heart of His character.

Where are we now?

Even if force is needed to repel extreme forms of tyranny like Adolf Hitler's Germany, Nicolae Ceauşescu's Romania or Radovan Karadzic's Bosnia-Herzegovina, the ultimate answer lies in the human heart and its rebirth through faith in the risen Christ; that is still the Christian message today, despite our chequered history. But what should our attitude be to this kingdom, that is, the authority structures in our own society? I have argued that it is a slight on God's character to suggest that He evaluates whether something is good or evil depending on what role the person committing the act holds in society. One of the reasons why the Psalms are so resonant with meaning for so many people is that they were written from the human perspective, not one of divine privilege, King David being the writer of many. Submission to authority seems formulaic, but what if more than one authority lays claim to the same jurisdiction? At one point in the Middle Ages three different people were laying claim to the Papacy; to obey one of them would meant disobeying the other two.

43. Romans 52:1-4.
44. Matthew 18:21-35.

St Paul's letter to the Romans explains that authorities are established by God but adds that 'the one in authority is God's servant for your good'.[45] The ruler is subject to God's authority as well because he or she is 'God's *servant*' [my emphasis]. Rulers do not have carte blanche to require obedience regardless of the nature of the command. So it is clear that submission to authority is not without condition; we as subjects are not expected to forgo normal moral expectations in order to comply with xenophobic, corrupt and murderous orders. To do so would exonerate the disciples for abandoning Christ at Calvary and leaving Him at the mercy of those Pharisees who were prepared to do anything to hold on to power. They did not all desert Him. John stayed with Christ during the crucifixion, as did Jesus' mother, his mother's sister, Mary, wife of Clopas, and Mary Magdalene.[46]

That we should not deny our faith seems incontrovertible, but if we live under a totalitarian regime and are threatened that our children will be abducted and sold into slavery unless we swear allegiance to the dictator and renounce our faith, what do we do? It is easy to criticise the disciples who ran away, but the question is this:

Q. What would I have done?

We should challenge injustice. If so, how should we? There is no easy answer in theory or practice; Christ did not leave one for us. We have the scriptures and our fellow believers, we have our consciences and we have our personal experience of faith. As we submit ourselves to God to ask what the right thing is to do in any situation, we have to discover what it is that needs to be done to enable others to have dignity, self-respect and a life without threat. Once we know what needs doing, then we have to work out how to do it, whether we are ruler or subject. Once

---

45. Romans 13:4.
46. John 19:25.

we know that, we have to work out the cost to ourselves and our loved ones and whether we are willing to bear it.

Chapter Two: Challenging Injustice

When we think something is unjust we often feel a sense of indignation. The trouble is that what strikes me as unjust might not necessarily trouble someone else. Do we all agree on what the greater injustice is when faced with alternatives? Take the following examples:

In our democracy, one person might think it unjust because the government is making people wear face masks in public, while another might believe it unfair that people are vulnerable to catch Covid-19 if mask-wearing is voluntary.

In a theocratic society, one person might feel that it is unjust for women to be deprived of the freedom to walk the streets with their faces covered, while another might feel it equally unjust to allow them to do so for religious reasons.

In a free market economy, one person might believe it unjust to be subject to a sudden high rent increase while the landlord might resent government restrictions on how much they can charge.

In a totalitarian regime, one person might feel it unjust to be deprived of the freedom to practise religion, while another might think it unjust not to punish disloyalty to the state.

From these examples, I hope it is clear that what we consider to be unjust is closely connected to the circumstances and the kind of society we find ourselves in. However, the disagreement is not just between societies, it is also within them. Ask an entrepreneur and a hotel domestic worker what they think injustice is and it is unlikely their answers will be the same. Where does the Christian start? The Old Testament prophet Isaiah makes it very clear:

Woe to those who make unjust laws,
to those who issue oppressive decrees,
to deprive the poor of their rights
and withhold justice from the oppressed of my people,
making widows their prey and robbing the fatherless.[47]

First of all, rulers who *make* unjust laws are responsible for their actions. Secondly, simply having a system of law does not satisfy the requirements of justice; unjust laws can be made, oppressive dictates can be issued. Thirdly, the failure to protect the vulnerable through *not* making effective laws is also a sin of omission. In these two verses we see three clear elements of justice.

1) Passing a law is not enough; its true purpose must be fulfilled.
2) One of the chief purposes of law is to ensure that the poor are not deprived of their rights.
3) The absence of effective justice will entail suffering for the vulnerable.

According to these principles, everyone should be valued and respected, but the experience of many individuals across the world does not bear this out in practice. In Britain, where I live, someone wrongly convicted of a crime can appeal to a higher court which independently reviews the evidence: someone in another country may live under a judiciary where the vast majority of legal decisions are based on bribery and partiality. A person in that kind of society would gladly settle for a fair legal system where *some* miscarriages of justice occur. An imperfect but largely independent judiciary is very different to a country where *all* the institutions are riddled with corruption. Someone else again might be living under a totalitarian system where there is not even the pretence

47. Isaiah 10:1-2.

of legality. The state enforcement of morality and loyalty is achieved through fear and punishment meted out by the police, the army, hired killers who are all fed by informers. It is an example of this kind of state that I want to now discuss.

The totalitarian state

Chengdu in Central China:

> Li Chengju glared at her prison interrogator as he pressed her to renounce her Christian church and condemn her pastor. Her captor warned she would not be so lucky as the pastor, who was locked in secret detention but at least might get a day in court. 'Look at you. You sweep the floors at church,' the interrogator said. 'You think you're getting a trial like your pastor? You don't qualify.'[48]

Since 2013 there has been an increase in the pressure put on churches to integrate Communist Party doctrine into the sermons given in church. As a rule, churches in China no longer meet in buildings, preferring to meet in smaller groups in the homes of the believers. Christians in China carry out their faith knowing that the authorities disapprove and could turn against them in a brutal and destructive way. It is no surprise that under such pressure many will set their eyes on the kingdom of heaven rather than the kingdom of God here on earth. What might be normal activities in a Western democracy, such as evangelism, meeting for worship, pilgrimage, social action in the community and liaising with state services about vulnerable individuals are all off limits when

---

48. Alice Su, 'For China's Underground Churches, this was no easy Christmas', *Los Angeles Times*, 25 December 2019. See www.latimes.com/world-nation/story/2019-12-25/china-church-sinicization (accessed 19 July 2021).

living under a regime that thrives on blind obedience. Even Christians, however, are not being held, en masse, in detention camps.

Xinjiang in North West China:

In 2009 about 200 people died in clashes in Xinjiang, which the Chinese blamed on Uyghur Muslims who wanted their own state. But in recent years a massive security crackdown has crushed dissent; 're-education' camps have been introduced. In 2017, President Xi Jinping issued an order saying all religions in China should be Chinese in orientation. People who have managed to escape the camps have reported physical, mental and sexual torture. Women have spoken of mass rape and sexual abuse. China says the crackdown in Xinjiang is necessary to prevent terrorism and root out Islamist extremism and the camps are an effective tool for re-educating inmates in its fight against terrorism.[49]

It is important to consider the economic significance of Xinjiang, where the majority of the Uighur Muslims live. It is the home of 'China's largest gas fields, half its coal deposits and as much as a fifth of its oil reserves'.[50] I was surprised to discover where some of the foreign investment assisting China's control of its population comes from. Cisco, the US multinational company, provided China with 'hardware for mass video surveillance in Chongqing' in Central China in 2011. In 2017 Deutsche Bank recommended its shareholders to invest in companies that would provide surveillance equipment and software for the authorities in

---

49. 'Who are the Uyghurs and why is China being accused of genocide?' BBC News, 21st June 2021. See www.bbc.co.uk/news/world-asia-china-22278037 (accessed 21 July 2021). Please note that 'Uyghur' can also be spelt 'Uighur'.
50. Peter Frankopan, *The New Silk Roads: The Present and Future of the World* (London: Bloomsbury Publishing, 2019), p. 103

Xinjiang.[51] The Chinese government have also been concerned about Uighur Muslims being recruited to fight for Islamic State and made links with the Taliban prior to the US withdrawal of troops from Afghanistan in the summer of 2021.[52] The persecution of the Uighur Muslims is politically and economically as well as ideologically motivated.

In 2019 the *Church Times* reported the following statement by Dr Alan Smith, bishop of St Albans:

> The Chinese government thinks that it can 'fool the international community' and get away with injust [sic] treatment of religious minorities … He described the treatment of Uighur Muslims in the Xinjiang region as 'the latest example of the systematic crack down on religious minorities by the Chinese government.
>
> 'As well as the detention camps for Uighur Muslims in Xinjiang Province, and the demolition of Christian churches in Shanxi, the Chinese have also opened up camps, euphemistically called "vocational schools", for Buddhists, in Tibet.
>
> 'I am glad to add my voice to religious and political leaders around the world to speak out against this oppression and protect these persecuted minorities.'[53]

In August 2020, eighty-one leaders from Christian, Jewish, Buddhist and Muslim communities signed a joint letter comparing the Uyghur problem as being equivalent to Hitler's persecution of the Jews in the 1930s:

---

51. Op. cit. p. 105.

52. Op. cit. pp. 103, 107.

53. Madeleine Davies, 'Bishop speaks out on treatment of Uighur Muslims in China', Church Times, 16th August 2019, https://www.churchtimes.co.uk/articles/2019/16-august/news/world/bishop-speaks-out-on-treatment-of-uighur-muslims-in-china (accessed 26 July 2021).

In the Holocaust some Christians rescued Jews. Some spoke out. To quote Dietrich Bonhoeffer, 'Silence in the face of evil is itself evil … Not to speak is to speak. Not to act is to act'. After the Holocaust, the world said 'Never Again.' Today, we repeat those words 'Never Again', all over again. We stand with the Uyghurs. We also stand with Tibetan Buddhists, Falun Gong practitioners and Christians throughout China who face the worst crackdown on freedom of religion or belief since the Cultural Revolution.[54]

What should Christians do? Dietrich Bonhoeffer was not Jewish, yet he spoke out for their right of human dignity. Christians are not Muslims, Tibetan Buddhists or Falun Gong practitioners, but surely we should speak out for their rights, including the freedom to practise religion. North West China is many miles and many worlds away from us, but we cannot turn a blind eye to such wrongdoing; our voices should be heard along with others.[55] At the UN in October 2020, thirty-nine countries condemned China's treatment of the Uighurs but *forty-five* did not.

There appear to be a number of reasons why there are limited voices from Muslim countries about the plight of the Uighur Muslims in North West China. The Chinese authorities have imposed a *1984*-style[56] news blockade on what is actually happening in the Xinjiang region and they have invested heavily in many majority Muslim countries. Some, like Saudi Arabia, mirror the totalitarian aspects of the Chinese regime

---

54. 'Archbishop Rowan Williams joins faith leaders demanding justice for China's Uyghurs'. Press release 10 August 2020, https://anglican.ink/2020/08/10/archbishop-rowan-williams-joins-faith-leaders-demanding-justice-for-chinas-uyghurs/ (accessed 10 August 2020).

55. Margaret Besheer, 'VOA news on China At UN: 39 Countries Condemn China's Abuses of Uighurs', 6 October 2020. See www.voanews.com/east-asia-pacific/voa-news-china/un-39-countries-condemn-chinas-abuses-uighurs (accessed 29 November 2021). Thirty-nine countries condemned China's treatment of the Uyghurs while forty-five countries endorsed it as legitimate in counteracting terrorism.

56. A reference to George Orwell's futuristic novel.

in their own countries; others are too indebted to speak out, such as Pakistan. The influence of the Chinese economy in the world today is far, far greater than the influence of the German economy in the 1930s and so combating such injustice requires a combination of individual bravery as well as universal international cooperation, something which does not currently exist at a level where change can be effected.[57] There can be a cost; for those like Rushan Abbas, director, Campaign for Uyghurs, who spoke out against the brutality, her sister disappeared six days later and she had not heard from her for almost a year when speaking in an Al Jazeera broadcast on 12 August 2019.[58]

Q. When Western governments condemn the human rights abuses which are taking place in China, should they also condemn Western companies for investing in Chinese surveillance equipment?

Freedom of conscience

The question of whether Christ advocated for freedom of conscience is one that, at first glance, does not appear to be directly referred to in the gospel accounts. However, the story of Christ's trial provides an answer.

Jesus asked the officers of the Temple Guard and the elders who had come for him, 'Am I leading a rebellion, that you have come with swords and clubs?'[59] He had just told his followers not to use the sword and

---

57. Please see 'Have Muslim countries abandoned Chinese Uighurs?' Al Jazeera Live Stream. See www.bing.com/videos/search?q=which+religious+groups+have+spoken+out+about+the+uyghur+muslims+in+china&docid=608052633485007562&mid=A1B8770002996B9D920DA1B8770002996B9D920D&view (accessed 27 July 2021).

58 'Archbishop Rowan Williams joins faith leaders demanding justice for China's Uyghurs'. Press release 10 August 2020, https://anglican.ink/2020/08/10/archbishop-rowan-williams-joins-faith-leaders-demanding-justice-for-chinas-uyghurs/ (accessed 10 August 2020).

59. Luke 22:52.

healed the high priest's servant's ear after what must have been an angry confrontation. He was then taken to the house of the high priest and the next morning brought before the chief priests and the teachers of the law. They questioned Him as to whether He was the Son of God and He said He was.[60]

This blasphemy, as they saw it, immediately led them to take Jesus to Pilate. They said, 'We have found this man subverting our nation. He opposes payment of taxes to Caesar and claims to be Messiah, a king.'[61] Pilate's passed the problem to Herod because Jesus was Galilean. Despite taunting Him, Herod sent Jesus back to Pilate who repeatedly told the Jewish leaders that he could 'find no basis for a charge against him'.[62] Eventually Pilate gave way to their demands and Jesus was led away by the Roman soldiers to be crucified.

The real pressure point for the Jewish leaders was that Christ threatened their authority and legitimacy by claiming to be the Saviour, the one who was to come. However, when they went to Pilate the *first* thing they said was that Christ was 'subverting our nation' and encouraging the non-payment of tax, even though they knew that Jesus had recently said that they should 'give ... to Caesar what is Caesar's'.[63] Rather, they told Pilate what they thought would make him convict Christ *regardless* of the facts.

Without doubt, the trial of Christ was a contrivance for the purpose of the Jewish leaders holding onto power and as such, Christ's claims were not respected but used against Him. Any consideration of Christ being free to state His convictions was swallowed up by the fact that He was seen as a threat to the status quo. If Christ's freedom of conscience

60. Luke 22:66-70
61. Luke 23:1-2.
62. John 18:38; 19:4,6.
63. Luke 20:20-25.

was abused in order to have Him killed, then not to allow freedom of conscience must be wrong.

Should the Uyghur Muslims and other minorities be subjected to a similar contrivance that Christ was subject to in order for the Chinese state authorities to maintain political control? Christians will not agree with Islamic and other doctrines, but surely we must reject the treatment of Muslims or anyone else in the way that Christ was dealt with. As Dietrich Bonhoeffer said, 'Not to speak is to speak. Not to act is to act.'[64]

Q. What are the limits of freedom of conscience? Why is bullying, harassment and intimidation outside the remit of freedom of conscience?

The point of this question is to suggest that freedom of conscience has limits if that freedom is misused to damage others, but that it should not be restricted for the purpose of gaining or maintaining political control. Christ's freedom of conscience was restricted so the Pharisees could maintain their stronghold over the Jewish community.

A broken society – corruption, fear and land grab in El Salvador

There is a sharp contrast between a totalitarian regime where the state seeks to exert control over minds and hearts and a society which has a history where democratic processes are subverted by a competition for power between elites, including the military. El Salvador's history is a telling example.

In 1524 the Pipils who had lived in El Salvador since the eleventh century were displaced by a Spanish invasion. They took the Pipils'

---

64. 'Archbishop Rowan Williams joins faith leaders demanding justice for China's Uyghurs'. Press release 10 August 2020, https://anglican.ink/2020/08/10/archbishop-rowan-williams-joins-faith-leaders-demanding-justice-for-chinas-uyghurs/ (accessed 10 August 2020).

land and the indigenous population shrank. By 1800, several families controlled half the land in the country. The indigenous populations who grew crops for export in return for very low wages were controlled by these Spanish families. Although El Salvador gained a form of independence from Spain in 1821, it was not until the failed United Provinces of Central America collapsed in 1840 that full autonomy was achieved. Political chaos followed and in the 1860s coffee-growing replaced indigo as the main export crop. The 'fourteen families', as they were known, continued to 'rule the destinies of the Salvadoran state until the early decades of the 20th century and beyond'.[65]

In 1931, Communist party members were told they were not eligible to stand in national elections; in any event, the victorious candidate was replaced by a government-run militia. This military junta then allowed Communists to stand, but subsequently cancelled their victories at the polls. A revolt was put down in a massacre known as 'La Matanza' which means 'slaughter'. A period of repression followed.

A resistance movement, the FMNL (Farabundo Marti Liberation Front), was formed and received financial support from Cuba. The government received aid from the United States to counteract it. Attempts to create a fair society failed. José Duarte, a Christian democrat, won a landslide election in 1972 but was prevented from taking office, tortured and exiled. In 1979, a government made up of both military and civilian personnel attempted to broker peace, but soon reverted to repressive methods as they clashed with both the far right and far left.

Archbishop Óscar Romero, who had for several years been reluctant to engage with the politics of the country, became convinced that he should stand up for the dispossessed and the poor; he opposed the brutality and killing by the military and the death squads in the pay of the elites. He wrote to President Carter asking for US aid to be stopped

---

65. Carlos R. Colindres, El Salvador Today (Great Britain: Amazon, 2020), pp. 66-69.

as it was reinforcing the oppressive and murderous acts carried out by those in government. He appealed to the military as well. A week later on 24 March 1980 he was murdered while saying mass at a hospital chapel. No one was ever convicted of the crime. Soon after, a full-scale civil war raged for twelve years, but even when peace was brokered, scars did not heal easily. Marigold Best and Pamela Hussey relate a story of some women who had been betrayed to the militia by a little old woman during the civil war but forgave her because they knew she needed food for her family. They ended up supporting her. However, when the political party in power drove past they shouted at them calling them murderers.[66] They could forgive the little old lady but not the regime who they believed were the true perpetrators of the suffering they had had to endure.

The work of Christian Aid in 2020 illustrates that deep problems remain within El Salvador:

> We work with poor families in rural, semi-urban and urban communities who are marginalised, landless or living at subsistence level – prioritising women, youth and ethnic groups who have historically been excluded and discriminated against.[67]

There are some signs that the extremes of poverty are decreasing, but nowhere near disappearing.[68] The dominance of two rival gangs, MS-13 and 18th Street across Central America and the US, is perhaps the greatest visible barrier to the growth of civil society today.[69]

---

66. Marigold Best and Pamela Hussey, *A Culture of Peace, Women, Faith and Reconciliation* (London: Catholic Institute for International Relations, 2005), p. 8.

67. 'Christian Aid in El Salvador'. See www.christianaid.org.uk/our-work/where-we-work/el-salvador (accessed 26 July 2021).

68. See 'World Bank in El Salvador' overview, 9 October 2020, www.worldbank.org/en/country/elsalvador/overview (accessed on 2 August 2021).

69. Colindres, *El Salvador Today*, pp. 86-93. Please also see Chapter 4 for a detailed account of recent history.

Liberation theology

During the civil war, the theology of liberation was *one part* of the Catholic Church's reaction to widespread corruption and violence. Essentially in the cauldron of El Salvador, some Catholic priests substituted Christian theology with Marxist ideology, claiming that violent class struggle was the only way to fight for justice. Archbishop Óscar Romero was wrongly associated with such an approach. In condemning the threat made against the Jesuits, that they would be killed within thirty days if they did not leave El Salvador, he said this:

> The only violence that Jesus allows is the violence that he himself is going to suffer: giving his blood, letting himself be assaulted and killed, because only his blood can give life to the world. There is no other blood that can be legitimately shed apart from that which love poured out to save us.[70]

Violence was not the means to achieve social reform. Shortly before the threat against the Jesuits was made, the corpse of politician Dr Mauricio Borgonovo Pohl had been discovered twenty days after his kidnap in May 1977. Romero said this at his funeral mass:

> At this time, in front of the body of our beloved foreign minister, I repeat once more: violence is not Christian; violence is not human; nothing violent can long endure.[71]

---

70. 'St Oscar Romero, Homily for 13th Sunday of Ordinary Time (Year C), 26 June 1977 Responsibility for God's Kingdom', www.romerotrust.org.uk/homilies-and-writings/homilies/responsibility-gods-kingdom (accessed 3 August 2021).

71. See 'The Church Before Grief & Violence, Funeral of Chancellor, Mauricio Borgonovo', Wednesday, 11 May 1977, www.romerotrust.org.uk/homilies-and-writings/homilies/church-grief-violence (accessed 4 August 2021).

What Archbishop Romero advocated for was faithfulness to the primacy of faith in Christ and the courage to condemn the forces which put human dignity in second place; the two went together. He did this knowing that his own life would be placed at risk. He felt that Marxist ideology with its emphasis on material reality excluded the spiritual and that the capitalist preoccupation with profit did exactly the same thing.[72]

Archbishop Romero's legacy was recently celebrated on 24 March 2021. Archbishop Jose Luis Escobar Alas of San Salvador said that 'Salvadorans face an unjust system of "spurious laws" that, "far from protecting the vulnerable and weak, protect capital, delinquency and corruption." Romero, he said, 'would ask for reform of the social security or pension benefits, tax codes, the rights of workers, migrants and women – all groups whose difficulties have become even more pronounced during the pandemic'.[73]

The situation in El Salvador today is still grave, as it is in so many other countries around the globe. It may not be a rigid totalitarian state in the same way that China is, but it is still a broken society. When the bullets stop, the memories do not; when militias are replaced by governmental structures, corruption does not vanish, and when priests are murdered, investigations do not automatically become free from political influence.

---

72. In this homily given on 22 May 1977 ,'The Violence that Saddens the Country', Romero refers to several recent violent deaths and the occupation on 19 May 1977 of the church in Aguilares by members of the Armed Forces and the National Guard and their expulsion of the Jesuit community. See www.romerotrust.org.uk/homilies-and-writings/homilies/violence-saddens-country (accessed 3 August 2021).

73. Rhina Guidos, Catholic News Service, 'Despite pandemic and strife, El Salvador gathers to remember St Romero', 26March 2021. See https://cruxnow.com/church-in-the-americas/2021/03/despite-pandemic-and-strife-el-salvador-gathers-to-remember-st-romero/ (accessed 3 August 2021).

Three pictures of Christ

In the middle of such fear, it is hard to know what we would do if we were in the same position. How would we respond to the threat that our families would be kidnapped, killed or abused if we did not comply with the demands of groups of soldiers, death squads or government officials?

I do not know the answer as to how I would respond, but it is clear that God's love, if it is true, cannot remain behind closed doors when it comes to speaking out for the dispossessed. There are three ways of looking at Christ which may be helpful:

1. The broken Christ: this is Christ in the garden telling His Father of the pain He would rather not endure, but even so, He would follow His Father's will. This is the innocent sufferer, the persecuted and the person whose life is being cut short. This is His mother looking on, helpless, and this is the brutality of power seekers whose only remedy is to murder, twist the facts and justify their own actions to themselves.

2. The risen Christ: this is the startled disbelief of the disciples as they begin to come out of hiding, ready to spread the good news that Christ has overcome the chaos created by murder, deceit, brutality, neglect, hate and death itself.

3. The human Christ: this is the advocate of the poor and the bullied and those taken advantage of by greed in the workplace and the home. It is the Christ that notices the person that no one else notices, who speaks against the hypocrisy of those who wield power for their own benefit and who sell harmful drugs for profit. It is the Christ who represents the victim and challenges the perpetrator; it is the Christ who brings His Father's *character* into the world.

In societies like El Salvador, all three perspectives are relevant for Christians. In Western democracies such as our own, we need to ask if we have become anaesthetised to the ills on our doorstep. I live in a comfortable area, go to a church which is not persecuted, where the gospel is preached and the power of community reaches out to people in need. But in the same city that I live in there are drug gangs, rough sleepers, isolated elderly people who suffer with Alzheimer's disease, women fearing to walk the streets alone, knife crime, food banks and a whole host of people barely making ends meet. I know they are there, I give to agencies which try to offer support, but I have come to accept the status quo. The Church in a post-Christian, relatively affluent society has to ask itself whether it is content with that status quo.

Q. If the ingredients needed to challenge wrongdoing and brokenness are courage, humility and faith, how should the accusation of being politically naïve be met?

Chapter Three: Living in a Secular Culture

How do we move from a place where we *instantly know* what injustice is – a place where people are indiscriminately brutalised by criminal gangs, or subject to the murderous threats by the police in totalitarian regimes – to where people are scratching their heads as to what *counts* as injustice?

Some think the extremes of wealth and poverty constitute evidence of injustice; others do not. Some consider that it is acceptable to use tax havens to accumulate wealth, if you can get away with it; others protest. Some consider equalities to be vital, while others believe that such rigid expectations deprive people of the right to free speech. Some think that legalising assisted dying is unjust, when others equally believe it wrong to criminalise it; the list goes on. How, in this maze of differing perspectives, can anyone say what injustice actually is?

Modern ways of thinking explain justice in a way which does not rely on any God-based theories. Excluding God leaves us with two alternatives: does nature shape our sense of justice or are we free to make up whatever system we want?

Theories of nature say we are a product of the material world, not just as babies, but also as social and political creatures in adulthood. The theory of evolution has influenced our view of how nature works: protecting the young of a species, living in small groups where roles are allocated to men and women, hunting while protecting the group from outside attack are all contributory factors which have formed our natural human psychology over hundreds of thousands of years. Modern concepts like 'justice' and 'punishment' have emerged from such primitive beginnings.

An alternative approach says that people are more or less free to decide what sort of society they want to construct for themselves. This idea has grown the more society has departed from traditional ways of living. For example, we now know that women are not biologically consigned to be 'homemakers', kept by their male breadwinner; what was once thought of as unchangeable is not so any more.

We start with the first idea, 'nature'.

Natural Law

'Natural Law' refers to the predetermined *characteristics* of humanity. This approach maintains that the laws we make and live under are just another expression of *nature*. We humans are *part of* nature and therefore have certain traits that belong to our species. We might say that all dogs exhibit 'dog-like' behaviour, even though there are different breeds of dog; human beings, similarly, have common traits, even though every individual is unique.

However, in *each* individual those common traits are arranged in a unique way. Any dog owner will say that different dogs have different temperaments. Any parent will know that no two children are alike. Any observer of different communities, cultures and societies will make the same observation. The more questions we ask about our basic nature, the more complex the answer becomes. So are we naturally communal or naturally private? Are we naturally trusting or naturally suspicious? Are we naturally selfish or naturally altruistic? Are we naturally consistent or naturally fickle? We all, psychopaths apart, have moral sensibilities, but mine are arranged differently to yours. So the question arises as to what comes first: nurture or suspicion, care or aggression, community or self? Two major Enlightenment political philosophers, Thomas Hobbes and John Locke, provide a framework for reflection.

Thomas Hobbes' (1588-1679) political philosophy was based on the primacy of fear and insecurity; we are so afraid of others taking advantage of us that we would rather sign up to being under an unjust government than being subject to a weak and transient one. Thomas Hobbes would have preferred the stability offered by a totalitarian regime to the insecurity of a corrupt one. That may have been true for him, but his theory was that we *all* think in that same way.

John Locke (1632-1704), on the other hand, starts from a position where human goodness is imparted to us from God through creation. Even though Locke derived his view of our natures from his belief in God, his political theory was primarily about moving the relationship between government and the governed from an autocratic dominance to a contractually based arrangement. Our good natures are spoilt by our failings and so we have to organise a government which will restrain the more destructive aspects of our behaviour. Our natural instinct is aimed towards goodness, so the governments we appoint should be neither totalitarian nor corrupt; they should serve the people as well as be masters of them. Locke is one of the founders of modern democratic theory. Both Locke and Hobbes relied on nature to inform their political theories, but they had very different conceptions about which of our instincts, fear or trust, prevail.

Q. Is your first instinct to trust a stranger, or be wary of them? Whatever your answer is, does it help you further your understanding of human nature?

Nature provides part of our understanding when it comes to how societies work, but is it a complete explanation? A person who is much more *naturally* inclined to anger may exercise a great deal more *moral restraint* than someone who is naturally calm and unruffled. For me, a nagging doubt remains as to whether justice, despite its misuse and inadequacy, is ultimately *only* a device which has emerged to curb the more negative aspects of human behaviour. When an injustice is put right, I feel that something greater than a containment of anti-social behaviour is present.

Tim Keller sets out to show what justice looks like when God used the prophets in the Old Testament as His mouthpiece. In Keller's analysis, the proper balance between retributive justice, that is, justice which punishes wrongdoing, and restorative justice, the repair of neglect and deprivation, is central to God's *character*. Justice is more than the righting of wrongs; it is God's vision of how His essence can be reflected in human society. Justice is as much about 'grace and compassion' as it is about the 'action' needed to protect rights for all.[74] Institutional 'action' without sufficient common 'grace and compassion' leaves a deep uncertainty about the force of the moral imperative which should motivate us to keep the rules: if we only have rules and no overarching motivation to keep them, then rule-bending for self-interested purposes seems very tempting. Christ summed up the impact of combining love with law when He answered this question:

Hearing that Jesus had silenced the Sadducees, the Pharisees got together. One of them, an expert in the law, tested him with this question: "Teacher, which is the greatest commandment in the Law?" Jesus replied: "'Love the Lord your God with all your heart and with all your soul and with all your mind.' This is the first and greatest commandment. And the second is like it: 'Love your neighbour as yourself.' *All the Law and the Prophets hang on these two commandments.*"[75]

---

74. Timothy Keller, *Generous Justice* (London: Hodder & Stoughton, 2010), p. 3.
75. Matthew 22:34-40, my emphasis.

The picture in Mosaic Law is where individual purpose and the well-being of society are intertwined. While there is scope for individuals to acquire wealth, the rules of gleaning (making provision for the poor), debt relief, tithing (taxation) and the Jubilee (a periodic return of land to the original holders) are all insurances against the extremes of wealth and poverty becoming immovable.[76] God is named as the God of 'the fatherless' and a 'defender of widows' and not the God of the rich and powerful.[77] This was the vision; the reality was, of course, something else.

From a biblical perspective, without a cultural norm of 'grace and compassion', justice is incomplete. This does not only apply to poverty, but also the general way relationships are conducted. I was wondering how to illustrate this when in August 2021, this happened:[78]

My wife and I were having lunch in the open air at a local café near some woods. It was very sunny and pleasant with around twenty-five people sitting outside. Suddenly an argument blew up. Someone had seen a dog walking along a nearby path with a trailing lead on the ground. They approached a man and asked him if it was his dog and he gave an abrupt answer indicating that it was nothing to concern them. The person became consumed with anger, shouting, and it looked at one stage as if it would end up becoming physical. They stood back after a while, still shouting that the man shouldn't swear in front of a child. Everyone was taken aback by the ferocity of the argument. The man walked off and then the aggrieved person phoned the police to complain, giving them a description of the man – it seemed he had been seen going back to his vehicle and was leaving the woods. After we

---

76. Keller, *Generous Justice*, p. 32.
77. Op cit. p. 6. See Psalm 68:4-5.
78. I wrote this summary the day after.

finished lunch, we drove up the road to find three police vehicles and an ambulance with the man on the ground, handcuffed! The police had approached him and he had ended up hitting one of them. He was arrested and his vehicle and his dog were taken possession of.

What struck me from witnessing this sorry incident was that the law could only deal with the physical assault. The other issues, including the surly response from the man, the disproportionate anger of the complainant and the needs of the child could not be dealt with by the 'justice' system, but they were essential parts of the story. However one might characterise it, the law regarding assault could not make up for the absence of 'grace and compassion' which would have averted the situation arising in the first place. 'The Bible teaches that the sacredness of God has in some ways been imparted to humanity, so that every human life is sacred and every human being has dignity.'[79] Tim Keller argues that the erratic appearance of natural grace in our interactions with others is where the redemptive grace of Christ is needed to recapture God's original intention for us, both as individuals and for society: 'Grace makes you just.'[80] The vision and the reality are not the same, but with no vision the reality fades.

Q. Families of victims who are indiscriminately murdered sometimes come out of court to say that justice has been done; they all say that nothing can replace their loved one. Does this, a poignant example of the absence of 'grace and compassion', illustrate Tim Keller's description of divine justice?

79. Keller, *Generous Justice*, p. 83.
80. Op. cit. p. 99.

Positive Law

'Positive Law', in contrast to 'Natural Law', is a way of saying that societies are entitled to make up their own rules. [81] In fact, when societies rely on external or 'divine' revelation they can end up following rules they don't understand which can then be used by those in power to abuse an unsuspecting populace. The course of Medieval and Renaissance European history reveals many examples of this but equally, modern democratic politics and financial regulatory bodies are awash with issues about conflicts of interests, double standards and insider trading. No society is free from corrupt and dishonest practice. However, 'Positive Law' is not simply about throwing 'God' out of the equation; it is the claim that the fixed points of nature, as we see them, can be changed. Nature is malleable and can be moulded to suit our needs. Our DNA used to control us, now we control it; that is the direction secular thinking is now moving in.

In the modern age, democratic societies have increasingly adopted 'Positive Law' approaches in order to escape from past draconian methods of enforcing traditional sexual morality. 'Equalities' and their enshrinement in law are sometimes portrayed as the measure of moral progress. They cut across traditional forms of family life and are held up as examples of the way we can construct our own laws to suit our changing attitudes. 'Equalities' are generally thought to be underpinned by the principle of 'equal respect for every individual'. [82] If equal respect applies to *all*, then no society is exempt; without realising it, a *universal* moral principle is covertly smuggled into the rationale which supports the 'equalities' agenda. This is a problem, because if societies *are* free

---

81. Totalitarian societies also make laws as means of maintaining political and military control, but the term 'positive law' is generally confined to the democratic context.

82. Please see Ronald Dworkin's reference to John Rawl's view of 'human beings as moral persons' in *Taking Rights Seriously* (London: Duckworth, 1977), p. 181.

to dispense with traditional family and gender beliefs they are *not* free to do anything which prevents everyone from being equally respected. Even in the furthest rebuttal of traditional family structures there is a restraining element if respect for *all* is to be included.

In personal relationships we respect others to varying degrees, depending on what we think about their behaviour, attitude and the way they treat us. Nevertheless, we expect laws *not* to discriminate against individuals on the basis of their personal moral qualities. Imagine two people are being tried for theft: one is very rude and critical of people, while the other is polite and considerate in manner. The law should try them *equally* as far as the evidence is concerned; to include an assessment of their character into the case would mean they were not being tried for theft alone but also for the sort of person they were. If the legal system is based on impartiality, courts cannot take into account whether or not they find the defendant attractive, personable, upright and even of good company. Equal consideration under the law is not the same as equal respect in ordinary social and commercial relationships. In law it is about *excluding* factors which could lead to a biased and unfair outcome, so I can be verbally abusive, uncooperative and sulky but still be discriminated against. The law examines specific *parts* of a person's behaviour not their *whole* lives.

On one hand, when there is an absence of common respect, legal cases increasingly move towards being a competitive sport. However, when there are no restraining laws, the vulnerable are left with no protection at all, especially from those in positions of authority; crime goes unpunished. If the respect we show towards others is genuine it has to be grounded in a belief about their intrinsic value. The Utilitarian solution that every person deserves respect because society *works best* that way is unsatisfactory because we are left wondering whether we have to contrive or even feign respect in order to get the best out of our community. Schooldays remind us of being asked to show 'respect' that we didn't feel genuinely; effectively, we were simply being taught to be polite and civil.

Taking the situation I witnessed in the café, the police wanted to know whether a crime had been committed. The level of courtesy the man and the complainant showed to one another is a different aspect altogether. The way the argument affected the children in the vicinity is yet another dimension to explore. The incident had a number of different sides, but there is no doubt that had there been a greater degree of common respect, the result would have been very different.

So what is it that can justify intrinsic respect? To genuinely believe in respect we have to embrace the idea that other people have a value in themselves, even if their behaviour tells us otherwise. The idea of the intrinsic value of each person is not based on an assessment of their behaviour, honesty or trustworthiness, but on the belief that all individuals have potential to develop. People can become better at what they do, better at how they look after themselves and better at how they treat others. We derive much of our self-respect from the way we are cared for, particularly in childhood. It is because we have the potential to help or damage each other that we are valuable; as we *relate* to one another we can make a difference. Positive law initially offers the attraction, for many, of shedding outmoded traditional values. However, the problem remains that whatever *replaces* those traditional values will itself be value-laden, if it is to follow the principle of *equal respect for all*.

Q. What must it be like to live in a society where the universal principle of respect for all is ridiculed?

Modern democratic political perspectives: the right and the left

The balance between what is set for us by nature and what is open to change applies to contemporary politics as well as law-making, sexual ethics and everyday relationships. Have traditions been established and refined through the test of time, or are they a way of consolidating unfair power structures? Conservative political theory focuses on nature endowing people with different skills and levels of self-motivation; it is, therefore, mistaken to try to make everyone equal.

Alternatively, the left will claim that our natural state is one of shared dignity, and that we should use a certain degree of social construction (positive law) to ensure that the weak are not taken advantage of by the strong.

A typical view held by Conservatives of Labour views might run like this:[83]

1) Left-wingers are driven by sympathy for the underdog.

2) That sympathy is translated into government intervention to support the disadvantaged. Government intervention then provides a financial safety net for the unemployed and the unemployable.

3) However, too much reliance on government intervention leads to a dependency culture and higher tax rates for entrepreneurs. This reduces the incentives for those who make an active contribution to the economy. The result is apathy in the lower echelons of society, and so people lose the desire to become wealthy and economically self-sufficient.

---

83. In American politics, Republicans have some similarity to Conservatives, and Social Democrats have some similarity to Labour.

A typical view of Conservatives held by Labour supporters might run like this:

1) Right-wingers are driven by the need for individual autonomy, which is code for accumulating as much wealth as possible.

2) This aspiration for acquiring wealth requires the law to ensure that proper safeguards are in place to protect wealth and personal property.

3) This emphasis on the role of government as protector of private wealth leads to unacceptable inequalities in society and limited interventions to help the disadvantaged. The idea that society will get richer over time does not immediately prevent those at the bottom of the pile from experiencing hardship, poverty and unemployment. Welfare benefits are fundamentally there to prevent social disorder.

A supporter of the left might raise a faith-based argument along these lines: the basis of God's concern for the poor both in the Old Testament and in the life of Christ is akin to the desire parents have for *all* their offspring to live fulfilling lives. If three of your children are doing well and one of them is not, you naturally devote your energies to doing what you can for the child who is struggling while not neglecting the other two.[84] The parable of the lost sheep where the shepherd devotes his energies to finding one lost sheep out of 100 is an illustration of this principle.

A supporter of the right will, on the other hand, focus on the gift of freedom. Personal choice is central to the Christian account of God's dealing with humankind. The story of creation, the Fall and the

---

84. Keller, *Generous Justice*. See Chapters 1-5. See also the parable of the lost sheep: Luke 15:4-7.

subsequent separation between God and humanity shows how far God was prepared to go in order to offer us choice. The life, passion and resurrection of Christ is the ultimate sacrifice of a God who invites us to follow Him *or* not. *Choice* is integral to God's character, as much as righteousness, grace and justice.[85]

There are two biblical warning lights, one for the left and one for the right. For the left it is clear that much of Christ's teaching was about giving to others *voluntarily* rather than for effect or by compulsion. We know that Christ was aware of taxation systems, but He focused on *why* we give to those in need. It is because we want to see the receivers having their needs met rather than being seen in a good light ourselves and because we may have more than they do.

Be careful not to practise your righteousness in front of others to be seen by them. If you do, you will have no reward from your Father in heaven. So when you give to the needy, do not announce it with trumpets, as the hypocrites do in the synagogues and on the streets, to be honoured by others. Truly I tell you, they have received their reward in full.[86]

For the right, the gift of freedom is not a licence to create a society where the poor are left to their own devices while the rich have their assets protected through the law. As the story of the Fall demonstrates, the *way*

---

85. Many, including myself, have asked why God would take such a risk, the risk of creation going astray, if He is truly perfect. The most convincing answer to that question I have heard is that God is in essence, relational. It is in His nature to relate to others and the Trinity is a way of understanding how central that is to God's being and purpose. However, it is only God Himself coming into human life and entering into the darkest consequences and experiences of life, and rising again that enabled me to continue the journey of faith.

86. Matthew 6:1-2.

we use the gift of choice is critical. So what does God want us to use our autonomy for? The prophet Micah said this:

> And what does the LORD require of you?
> To act justly and to love mercy and to walk humbly with your God.[87]

The need for personal autonomy and sympathy for the underdog are not mutually exclusive; they are both fundamental characteristics of God. What does this mean in terms of modern right/left politics? If the use of personal autonomy is not solely reserved for personal economic advance but also used to work for the good of all, there is common ground as to what the outcome of policy should be. The way to get there will be in dispute. The left will favour strategies which involve taxation and redistribution while the right will prefer voluntary and charitable giving.

The Christian answer, hard though it may be to swallow, is that while ensuring we have enough to live on, we should focus on promoting reciprocity and not isolation. When Christ spoke of debtors in the Lord's Prayer, he was not just talking about Jewish debtors, he was talking about anyone.

> Give us today our daily bread
> Forgive us our debts,
> as we also have forgiven our debtors.[88]

It is, of course, the case that each Christian will have a different political viewpoint from the next when it comes to the extent of government's claim on our incomes in funding public services. The deeper question is

---

87. Micah 6:8.
88. Matthew 6:11-12.

how we should use our freedom and skills as 'living sacrifice[s]'[89] while 'looking [not only] to [our] own interests but ... [also] to the interests of ... others'.[90]

Whichever method is preferred, our political motives should be infused by Christ's summary of the Law and the Prophets, to love both God and our neighbours.[91] There has to be a way where the spiritual and moral outlook we derive from our faith feeds into both our political views and the way we express them. It is very easy, especially when emotions are running high, to reverse this sequence. The prophet Micah's words should help us to come back to earth when that happens. We should use our understanding of God's character to help us inform our approach to political life and the perspectives we hold, rather than determine what our political views are first and then look for supporting evidence from our faith to back those views up.

Q. For the Christian, how should political views connect to faith?

The problem of sexual ethics

The Church is in difficulty when it comes to sexual ethics. In 1964, Lord Devlin said this: 'I do not think there is anyone who asserts vocally that homosexuality is a good way of life but there may be those who believe it to be so.'[92] He was taking part in a debate regarding the decriminalisation of homosexuality; the Sexual Offences Act of 1967 began the process which took more than thirty years to complete. At the time of his well-

---

89. Romans 12:1.

90. Philippians 2:4.

91. Matthew 22:37-40.

92. Patrick Devlin, *The Enforcement of Morals* (Oxford: Oxford University Press, 1965), p. 116. The original lecture was delivered at the University of Chicago on 15 October 1964.

known debate with Professor H. L. A. Hart, Lord Devlin felt it was safe to assume that the vast majority were in favour of heterosexual marriage as the moral role model for family life.

He would have been astonished at the changes in attitudes which have occurred since then. Today, in order to be consistent, he would have had to say that most would accept homosexuality as a good way of life for those who identify themselves as lesbian or gay. His argument that society is held more firmly together if the law supports the moral consensus no longer holds for heterosexual marriage exclusively. He was assuming that things would not change, although he did think that the legalisation of homosexuality would unsettle the status quo.

There are existing laws against a variety of sexual offences. 'These crimes include domestic abuse, rape, sexual offences, stalking, harassment, so-called "honour-based" violence including forced marriage, female genital mutilation, child abuse, human trafficking focusing on sexual exploitation, prostitution, pornography and obscenity.'[93] However, there is no law against sexual acts conducted in private by consenting adults.

Christians are divided over the issue of accepting or challenging the new norm of acceptance when it comes to sexuality between consenting

93. Please see https://www.cps.gov.uk/crime-info/sexual-offences (accessed 16 August 2021).

adults.[94] Those who wish to challenge it do so because certain passages in the Bible explicitly forbid the practice, and that God made humankind male and female.[95] On the other hand, those who accept gay and lesbian people do not see the issue of sexuality as one of deliberate sinfulness but a result of nature's imprecision, and therefore see its condemnation as false moral superiority. The Church does not speak with one voice, as the tragic story of Lizzie Lowe demonstrates.

Lizzie Lowe was a fourteen-year-old girl who in 2014 took her own life because she could not reconcile being gay and being a Christian. She attended an evangelical church, but her parents were unaware of her struggles and would have accepted her had she told them about her worries. Her death, understandably, changed her church's approach to sexuality. It became inclusive, having previously been *silent* on the subject, at least from the pulpit. Some members of the congregation,

---

94. The issue of sexuality has been complicated further by the more recent arrival of gender politics. Here is a situation where gender can be fluid. The traditionalist view is that both gender and sexual orientation are physically determined by the way our bodies are made. Andrew Bunt says, 'Creation as male or female naturally flows into a commission to reproduce because it is our body's orientation towards reproduction that identifies us as male or female.' Andrew Bunt, *People Not Pronouns, Reflections on Transgender Experience* (Cambridge: Grove Books, 2021), p. 15. Whereas some secular approaches adopt a view that gender is fully the result of social construction, Andrew Bunt seems to adopt a view that gender feelings and emotions are fluid but our physical bodies are the only secure reference points for the determination of sexuality and gender. There are two resulting issues which cannot be fully discussed here: firstly, the existence of hermaphrodite individuals whose sexual organs are not clearly identifiable as male or female, and secondly, the fact that 'socially constructed' ideas have a neurological 'template'. Hence '… the exercise of autonomy and the influence of culture become embedded into our neurological memories.' Please see Nathan Driscoll, *The God Dilemma: A Philosophical Walk for the Undecided* (Welwyn Garden City: Malcolm Down, 2020), pp. 42-43. For my discussion on transgender issues please see Nathan Driscoll, *The Good Question* (Welwyn Garden City: Malcolm Down, 2021), pp. 109-111.

95. The extreme capital punishment for homosexuality in Leviticus 20:13 is *not* sought after by the proponents of those who consider the practice of homosexuality to be wrong.

however, did not feel they could continue to worship at the church and left.[96]

Those who take that traditional approach claim the right of free speech to continue to teach against the practice of same sex consensual relationships. In the current climate they are seen as holding a minority opinion in society at large and increasingly so in churches. Careful consideration needs to be given to ensure they are not vilified and subject to abuse.

There are, however, critical issues to face, most especially for teenagers like Lizzie Lowe. It is surely the priority to ensure that the tone of advice and guidance for young people is one that will not lead to such tragic outcomes. To take a completely different example, it is quite possible to vehemently preach against harbouring unkind thoughts towards others so as to make a young person feel so guilty that they may not believe they can be freed even if they are told they are forgiven by God. The *way* the gospel is preached can affect the vulnerable and the young in very different ways to those who are emotionally secure. We can preach the gospel in an open, reflective way that gives permission for doubt and genuine reflection; we can preach it in an overbearing, emotionally suffocating way that leaves the hearer with little room for manoeuvre.

There is also a wider canvas which appears to imply a 'moral' pecking order. Most churches do not exclude those who are divorced, or live together, or those who have had sex outside of marriage – these are all often considered to be in the *same category* as homosexuality when it comes to the traditional approach towards sexual relationships. Why, then, does homosexuality attract such a high profile? Is it being selected for special treatment? Christianity does have a great deal to say about relationships, and most of it is to do with loyalty, respect, forgiveness

---

96. Please see https://lizzielowe.org (accessed 16 August 2021).

and reconciliation. My view is that these weighty subjects are being lost in the sea of controversy over sexuality.

Those who want to preach about sexuality in a traditional context have to consider the safeguarding implications for their congregations, particularly the young and the vulnerable. There are enough cases of young people who identify as gay who have been brought up in traditional families; it is not possible to say that even the most conservative of Christians will not have to face up to their children growing up to say that they are gay. Some traditionalists who want heterosexual marriage to be the only option for family life may be reflecting on whether homosexuality should be recriminalised. If, as I believe, nothing positive would be gained from such a change, traditionalists have to then ask themselves how they would achieve the changes in behaviour and orientation they seek without causing harm.

Those Christians who are accepting of same-sex consensual relationships should focus on what is distinctively Christian about those relationships. What does Christianity have to say about the quality of relationships in a family context? How are Christian same-sex consensual relationships different from non-Christian ones? How does a Christian deal with prejudice, and how might our faith show itself when we challenge discrimination?

Christians on both sides of this divide have to face the fact that the 'world' sees a divided Church; can Christians work together to focus on the integrity, respect, compassion and honesty which is so needed in personal and institutional life? If we are not able to work together in this way, Paul's words that we 'are all one in Christ Jesus' will fall on deaf ears.[97] Most of the political questions around sexuality are political with a small 'p', because they are about how Christian leaders and pastors look after their congregations and how Christians work with

97. Galatians 3:28.

one another when they disagree on the issue of sexuality. 'Blessed are the peacemakers: for they shall be called the children of God.'[98]

Q. For the Christian, should sexual ethics be a matter of personal conscience or church policy?

The politics of institutions

We know from the account of creation and the Fall that God is not a totalitarian. We know from the story of Christ's 'trial' and crucifixion that God is not a friend of corrupt and self-serving rulers. And so we must ask how Christians who work in organisations, including the Church, can maintain the ethical standards that reflect what the Bible calls righteousness and what is known in the modern world as integrity?

Ignoring the unpopular

Sometimes it is easy to stand by and do nothing when someone is being scapegoated. Standing up for that person will involve a cost, perhaps a feeling of isolation or even being passed by for promotion. Even just talking with an unpopular person can make you wonder if you are being bad-mouthed. The power of the group is immense, as any school-aged child or young person will tell you. One thing Christ did was talk to people or pay attention to issues that His disciples did not think He should bother with.

> People were bringing little children to Jesus for him to place his hands on them, but the disciples rebuked them. When Jesus saw this, he was indignant. He said to them, 'Let the little children

---

98. Matthew 5:9, KJV.

come to me, and do not hinder them, for the kingdom of God belongs to such as these.'[99]

Deceitfulness

In management groups the culture of toughness, disregard of feelings and riding roughshod over people can often be the norm, while the public face of the organisation is one of politeness and charm. Double standards of behaviour become the acceptable way of working, but such an attitude betrays a fault line in the organisation that no decent person, Christian or otherwise, should consider acceptable. The language of Proverbs may be Victorian, but the meaning is unmistakable. There are seven things which are abominations to God:

haughty eyes,
a lying tongue,
hands that shed innocent blood,
a heart that devises wicked schemes,
feet that are quick to rush into evil,
a false witness who pours out lies
and a person who stirs up conflict in the community.[100]

Dishonesty

Illegal accounting practices sometimes conceal deeper problems, such as knowingly selling sub-standard products for inflated prices, paying staff wages which are impossible to live on, siphoning off large amounts of money for personal gain and political lobbying for self-interested purposes.

99. Mark 10:13-14.
100.Proverbs 6:17-19.

Do not have two differing weights in your bag – one heavy, one light. Do not have two differing measures in your house – one large, one small. You must have accurate and honest weights and measures, so that you may live long in the land the LORD YOUR GOD IS GIVING YOU.[101]

How difficult it is to stand up for honesty, decency and kindness when those around you are singing a different tune. Weighing up the cost of protesting or challenging, finding the emotional resources to do so and assessing the difficulties that might ensue for ourselves and those who are dependent on us fall heavily on us. How we should challenge is sometimes as difficult to work out as the challenge itself. What is for sure is that wherever we are, the way people are treated will be clear to see; we cannot close the door on it and sometimes we are compelled to do more than just look through the door.[102]

Q. How should leaders model integrity in their organisations?

101. Deuteronomy 25:13-15.
102. Do the following statements represent the organisation you work for or have a role in?

• People at all levels of the organisation are spoken to with the same level of respect.
• What is sold or provided is of good quality and customers and service users are not taken advantage of or short-changed.
• Where redundancies are being considered, those potentially affected are given due notice, appropriate financial advice and support.
• Working conditions and wages are fair, enabling workers to maintain a reasonable standard of living.
• Salary levels within the organisation reflect levels of responsibility undertaken, but are not at the extremes where some are disproportionately rewarded.

Interim Summary

The history of the Church shows us that Christians have either been completely separate from the state, closely aligned with it, or at other times somewhere in-between. During much of that time the spiritual focus of the Christian faith has been overtaken by political and territorial ambitions. I argue that rulers who describe their own political objectives as divinely approved claim something they are not entitled to claim; they are as bound by the moral and spiritual imperatives of the Christian faith as much as those they rule are.

God created humankind with the capacity to choose and so freedom of conscience is compatible with the way we conduct our relationships. Repressing the freedom to practice faith and replacing it with a compulsory and absolute requirement to show loyalty to the state is oppressive. Opposing dictatorship, corruption and threat requires courage to speak out for honesty and respect for the dignity of all, just as Christ did in His time on earth.

The impact of faith on political life should be to build a society where compassion, honesty and fairness underpin the institutions of society. The ingredients of nature's imprint and our capacity to decide for ourselves need the additional moral sense which comes from the principle of loving our neighbour as ourselves. For Christians, that moral sense derives from Christ's identification with human frailty and the opportunity we have to love God with all our heart and mind; moral sense is ultimately relational. Freedom should not be exclusively defined as an escape from existing cultural norms, but as an opportunity to respect and treat others fairly.

What's next?

The next two chapters are about democracy and theocracy respectively. In the West, democracy is the system we are most familiar with, even though many refugees will have come from living in oppressive regimes. However, it is a system that can be used in different ways by those elected into power; for example, in a self-serving way or with a more socially responsible approach. One of the difficulties is that what politicians say does not always reveal their true intentions. The chapter is written for you to reflect on what the limitations of democracy are and how principles of compassion, honesty and fairness can influence its nature.

The chapter on theocracy focuses on the difficulties which a government based on a single religion poses for those who do not follow that religion, or even those who do and want to practise it in a different way to the majority. It explores what such a system can imply for the level of political freedom in such a society, particularly when many different faiths are practised. The implications for Christians are obvious; is a government infused with the principles of honesty, compassion and fairness preferable to a theocratic 'Christian' government?

After these two chapters the conclusion to the book will follow.

Chapter Four: Democracy

What does democracy mean?

There are many different ideas about the meaning of democracy. For some, it is the opportunity to cast a vote; others want to actively participate in political life, while a significant number are disillusioned or simply feel powerless to exert any influence at all. We are all somewhere along the spectrum from intense political involvement to complete disaffection; for those who do engage, it is an opportunity to influence policy, choose a leader and keep political opponents at bay. Everyone will not get exactly what they hope for. Apart from the possibilities of being on the losing side, not being able to vote on each separate policy, and not necessarily liking the candidate we have voted for, there are many parts of our lives that democracy cannot reach. Democracy cannot determine the quality of our personal relationships, the personal meaning we look for in life and any preferred sense of community, even if we end up on the winning side of an election.

What can democracy deliver? Professor Alan Ryan outlines two broad ideas reflected by the writings of John Dewey and Joseph Schumpeter.[103] Dewey's type of democracy is not based so much on the electoral process as on the willingness of people to cooperate together to achieve shared aims. For Dewey, sitting on a committee with a number of like-minded people who are prepared to listen to a different point of view but share the *same* vision is the heart of democracy. Of course, committees are sometimes riven with conflict and dissension, but Dewey's vision is one of cooperation.

Schumpeter, on the other hand, sees democracy as a process which legitimises the rule of those who govern. He is more concerned about

---

103. Alan Ryan, *On Politics: A History of Political Thought From Heredotus to the Present* (London: Liveright Publishing Corporation, 2012), pp. 951-967.

the framework of rules than the interpretive meaning behind them. For him, fair election processes do not guarantee moral excellence or political competence or, for that matter, a general consensus, but without a robust framework, very little can get off the ground.

The way we use the idea of democracy is relevant to what we expect to get out of it. In a complex, multilayered society with financial, political, corporate and ideological interests, it is difficult to imagine how a comfortable sense of working amicably with a few others in running a sports club or setting up a church autumn fair can translate into the higher echelons of government. Where does that feeling of bonhomie go? Why does democracy end up with so many decisions being made by faceless civil servants or council officers?

The remoteness of governing elites means we do not know if politicians and officials are more interested in their personal ambitions than the needs of the citizens they are elected to serve. It is, not that easy to tell if a politician is guilty of self-interested manipulation or just being politically astute. We want to know what their basic motivations are.

Q. Can you think of any reasons why some go into politics with honourable intent and come out with tainted souls?

The following two views place the importance of 'trust' in very different places.

John Locke

John Locke believed that the only *absolute* authoritative relationship is one between God and human beings. Consequently, all human political relationships are negotiable and have to involve a significant element of consent between the rulers and the ruled. Governments can still exercise authority through punishment and sanction, but they are there for the *good* of the people, however that is understood. Even though people have very different opinions, Locke concluded that 'the law of nature ... is that measure God has set to the actions of men, for their mutual security ...'[104] In other words, the natural state of human beings is one of regard for one another: when we look out for each other, we satisfy our own natures. Locke placed the notion of trust in the centre of political life.

For Locke, the role of government is to preserve liberty, property and order. Should government step beyond that remit, then the people have a right to resist. Locke was writing at a time (the seventeenth century) when there were intense rivalries between the Catholic Church in Europe and the Protestant Church in England. Had his writings got into the wrong hands, he could easily have been subject to charges of insurrection, and potentially execution; he would have been accused of softening the sovereignty of the nation at a time when it needed to strengthen its defences. His approach was not simply to protect national security but to build a society based on a universally held moral consensus.

Machiavelli

When Niccolò Machiavelli (1469-1527) wrote his famous book *The Prince* he was effectively in political exile after a brief period as secretary to the Florentine Republic's 'Foreign Office' in the early part of the sixteenth century.

Machiavelli is often characterised as a political psychopath, but this perhaps overshadows how he thought about the more common aspirations held by the general population. He was not a politician who wanted to see bloodshed and chaos for its own sake. His principal aim

104. John Locke, *The First and Second Treatises of Government* (originally published anonymously in 1689, reprinted in Great Britain by Amazon), Second Treatise, Chapter II, point 8.

was to recapture the glory of a past Florence and, in particular, to advise a prince as to how he might achieve that.

What is chilling about Machiavelli's political strategy is that he advocated moving from honesty to dishonesty, kindness to cruelty, from peace to war and from love to hate in the blink of an eye. The astute politician would have no hesitation in resorting to amoral and immoral behaviour when it was required to sustain control. It would always be better for the population to enjoy stability, but if that stability was threatened, then the moral restraint of conscience was irrelevant. Machiavelli did not ever enact this philosophy, but it has caught the imagination of many who followed after him; they, unlike Locke, consider that human nature is best served by manipulating ordinary sentiments, religious or otherwise, in order to ensure military and political loyalty. The retention of personal political power by whatever means was the ultimate aim for the prince. Trust is a means to control, not an end in itself.

The kaleidoscope of democracy

Comparing John Locke's philosophy with that of Machiavelli leads us into some chilling waters; democracy can so easily be used as a means through which those who feed off power can manipulate their subjects. Some see human nature as essentially cooperative and some as a struggle for power, and presumably many are caught somewhere in-between, often depending on the situation. In Machiavelli's world, military power played a significant part in sustaining territorial control; in modern democracy, the mobilisation of sentiments through the media, the awarding of contracts to those in favour and the ability to borrow immense sums of money to fund particular projects are some of the weapons used to influence opinion.

The problem is not just one of how honest and upright politicians are. If the electorate are more attracted by charismatic figures than mundane ones, their voting preferences will not reflect choices about honesty and integrity. Rather, aspirations of identity, prosperity, self-determination and whatever else is put before us will prevail. In the same way that manufacturers are dependent on consumers for their income, so political parties are also dependent on voters for success at the polls. John Locke's theory applies equally to the governors and the governed, but it is the *nature* of the relationship between them which is crucial.

What sort of society do we want? To answer that question is no longer about negotiating a simple barter between privacy and community. If national self sufficiency is a priority, then the price of achieving it will most likely involve restrictions on foreign investment and that, in itself, may bring about a lower standard of living in the short to medium term. Environmental sustainability may also mean a reduction in living standards while new technologies are developed to the point where they are cost effective. If flowers, food products, mobile phone components and a host of other products and services are now sourced from the global marketplace, the question seems to be moving to 'what sort of world do we want' rather than 'what sort of society do we want'. The power of the individual is the power of the consumer; what do I buy and where is it made? Does my bank invest in the companies I approve of? How much do I need to live a comfortable life, and is there ever a point when I will stop wanting more and more expensive goods if, of course, I can afford them? Government policy is more likely to follow the material aspirations of individuals than create them; after all, politicians are elected by the people.

Q. Should I look to vote for the government that gives me the best financial deal, or which maximises the benefits for the least well off?

Liberal democracy

A Theory of Justice by philosopher John Rawls (1921-2002) is the most famous modern justification of liberal democracy; it is a theory which combines equal rights of liberty with agreed standards of material inequality. It is important to examine the key elements of his argument in order to place it into the context of the Christ's summary of the Law, namely to love God and also our neighbours as ourselves.

Democracy could be simply defined as the voice of the majority speaking through the ballot box; it is the means through which the ruling elites are chosen. What if the majority votes to oppress and murder a minority group in a brutal way? This is not an acceptable outcome, for two reasons. Firstly, such a move would effectively reduce the electorate to those who only supported one single point of view. Secondly, the system of democracy itself would have become a vehicle for murder.

How can such an outcome be avoided? Democracy can only be preserved if certain inalienable rights are accorded to each individual. Those rights protect political freedom, because voting to suppress and murder a minority group is voting to kill democracy itself. Once the idea of inalienable rights is introduced to the democratic ideal, some conception of the worth and dignity of each individual has also to be included. For the Christian, every single person is valuable in the sight of God.

a) Liberty

Broadly speaking, John Rawls felt everyone should be able to exercise freedom of thought and conscience, vote and participate in political life, hold personal property and be treated fairly and impartially under the law. These are the basic liberties for all. Rawls put it like this: 'Each person possesses an inviolability founded on justice that even the welfare of society as a whole cannot override.'[105] No popular vote should be allowed to compromise the basic liberties accorded to all citizens. Rawls accepted that when governments ignored those basic liberties, they should be challenged and resisted.[106]

Abraham Kuyper's 'confessional pluralism' is relevant here.[107] Kuyper (1837-1920) was a Dutch theologian and politician who maintained that different religious groups, interest groups and institutions should be accommodated *within* a democratic structure, even if the ideologies of some of those groups conflict with one another. The key idea behind this was that society should be robust enough to include groups which hold opposing ethical positions. The difficulty is judging how far a society can hold together in advance of such oppositions and defining what the boundaries are before the system of common consent disintegrates.

Q. Do social platforms encourage or restrict free speech?

This version of pluralism is currently under attack from the potential scope of Equalities legislation. So, for example, if an adoption agency wishes on the basis of its faith-based principles to restrict applicants to heterosexual couples, a legal question arises as to whether this is legitimate or not under the law. If anti-discrimination laws which apply to the *whole* of society prevent that adoption agency from functioning

105. John Rawls, *A Theory of Justice* (Oxford: Oxford University Press, 1971), p. 3.

106. Rawls, writing more than twenty years later, was concerned to emphasise that his conception of liberal democracy was essentially a political conception and not a moral one. He accepted that political conceptions are influenced by moral intuitions but did not want his theory to be held as the *only* version of liberal democracy; in this way he was able to say that his theory was not a barrier to pluralism. See Internet Encyclopedia of Philosophy, https://iep.utm.edu/rawls/ (accessed 1 September 2021).

107. Jonathan Chaplin, 'The Point of Kuyperian Pluralism, Facing exploitative capitalism and overweening statism, Kuyper's vision of pluralism should still inspire Christians today', *Comment*, 1 November 2013. See www.cardus.ca/comment/article/the-point-of-kuyperian-pluralism (accessed 15 September 2021).

in its preferred way, the extent of 'confessional pluralism' in society is necessarily diminished. If, however, the law only applied to public institutions, adoption agencies which are part of any government arm would *have* to allow both same-sex and heterosexual couples to apply, while religiously based private adoption agencies, should they choose to, would not.[108] This wider 'confessional pluralism' would involve a greater sense of agreeing to differ in popular culture.

At the heart of this debate is the question as to what should essentially be counted as a public or a private moral issue. If all public adoption agencies are *not* allowed to discriminate, should private adoption agencies be allowed to discriminate on the basis of their religious beliefs, even if those beliefs are objected to by the majority?

Philosopher John Stuart Mill (1806-73) said that what counts as immoral in one era can be transformed to one of moral acceptability in a subsequent one.[109] The issue of same-sex relationships is a case in point. Using Mill's principle that the only restraint on freedom is whether the exercise of it prevents others from exercising their own freedom, the question is this: if private adoption agencies are permitted to only accept applications from heterosexual couples while public ones are not, is harm being caused to same-sex couples who wish to adopt? In Kuyper's 'confessional pluralism' the answer is likely to be no, because same-sex couples are free to apply to public adoption agencies as well as those private ones who do not discriminate. Their right to apply for adoption

---

108. This discussion is not based on an actual case but see 'Court Rules that Evangelical Agency can Keep its Ethos', *Evangelical Times*, August 2020 at www.evangelical-times.org/news/court-rules-adoption-agency-can-keep-its-evangelical-ethos (accessed 19 September 2021). At the time of writing, the agency was permitted by the court to restrict applications to evangelicals only, but had to include same-sex couples by reason of its role in recruiting potential adopters for children who were the responsibility of local authorities. This ruling may have been appealed by the time of publication.

109. Devlin, *The Enforcement of Morals*, p. 108.

is not diminished, even though the number of agencies they can apply to is restricted.[110] Under this reasoning, private adoption agencies could only effect adoptions where potential adoptees were not previously in the care of public local authorities; that would restrict their pool of children to those of parents who approached the agency privately or came from overseas under the international adoption rules.

If the law is interpreted to mean that no such exemptions are permissible, then Mill's principle is replaced by a belief that the law should reflect a blanket moral expectation, as Lord Devlin argued in relation to heterosexual marriage in the 1960s. However, the substance of that blanket expectation has changed as it now *includes* same-sex relationships. Rawls says the general principle is that intolerance should be restricted up to the point where the basic securities of the tolerant and 'the institutions of liberty are in danger'.[111]

Q. How can we know if the basic securities of the tolerant and 'the institutions of liberty are in danger'?

b) Material inequality

Following his first principle concerning each individual's inviolable right to certain liberties, Rawls' second principle stated that economic and social inequalities should only exist if the advantages gained by some *also* benefit the least well off in that society.[112] Everyone should have the same opportunities, but some will inevitably make more money and social capital than others. John Rawls' initial 'veil of ignorance' where

---

110. There are also intermediate measures potentially available; for example, those private adoption agencies that choose not to assess same-sex couples could have a duty placed on them to direct and support same-sex couples to adoption agencies who would accept their application.

111. Rawls, *A Theory of Justice*, p. 220.

112. Op. cit. pp. 60-61.

individuals are asked to make up the rules of society without knowing where they would end up was a device which he thought would achieve a fair outcome; you would not want to devise rules where you could find yourself in the underclass. The theory was based on each society being a 'closed system isolated from other societies', which is not the reality of the global world we live in.[113]

The story of William Hartley (1846-1922) is an example of Rawls' second principle in action. He was the founder of Hartley's jam. He was innovative, entrepreneurial and honest, refusing to put substandard ingredients into the recipe, and selling at a fair price. He treated his employees with respect, even introducing a profit-sharing scheme for them because 'it seems to me right and doing as I would be done by.'[114] He built a garden village for his employees to live in and gave large donations for the construction of hospitals and extensions to the Primitive Methodists' theological college in Manchester. He used his liberty to practise his Christian faith, and his employees were in no doubt that they were benefiting from his entrepreneurial success.

Contrast this story with trying to apply the benefits of taxation and national insurance which all the income generators in a country 'give' to the least well off in that society. So how did the richest companies in the United Kingdom[115] benefit the 2,688 people estimated to be sleeping

---

113. Op. cit. p. 8. The globalisation of trade means that to be consistent with the principle of basic liberty, I should not buy any goods from nations who deprive parts of their population of those liberties. Rawls did make some later comments about the scope of interactions between democratic and non-democratic states, but for him there were definite limits as to how far democratic states should intervene in the functioning of non-democratic states. See Henry S. Richardson, 'John Rawls (1921-2002)'. See Internet Encyclopedia of Philosophy, https://iep.utm.edu/rawls/ (accessed 1 September 2021).

114. Peter Lupson, 'Jesus, Jam and a Christian Businessman', *Evangelicals Now*, August 2021, p. 25.

115. See www.economicshelp.org/finance/top-10-companies/ (accessed 24 August 2021).

rough on a single night in the autumn of 2020?[116] The question would mean nothing to the rough sleepers if they were asked, even if some calculation of tax redistribution and its effect was possible.

For people to *feel* the benefits, in the terms that Rawls uses, they have to *know* what good they are deriving from someone else's entrepreneurial success. It isn't simply that some have a job because companies need a labour force in order to operate. It isn't even about the workforce, because Rawls' second principle is about how the connection between material advantage and the *worst* off in society works; rough sleepers don't have a job. In order for society to feel like a community, the worst off should be able to *perceive* what the benefit to them accruing from someone else's economic success is. Towards the end of his life in 2002, Rawls observed how American society had moved away from the ideal of his second principle published in 1971.

Rawls' two principles were built around the idea of 'social cooperation among equals'.[117] But the hypothetical characters who devised the rules in his theory did not know where they would end up; there were no permanent *social ties* between them. They had no inclinations towards greed or jealousy, nor any history or traditions to draw on. Rawls' scheme is split between the twin themes of social cooperation and anonymity; the two do not sit easily together and that is why it is so hard to work out exactly how inequalities and redistribution through tax revenue contribute to social solidarity. If I receive unemployment benefit because people richer than I pay taxes, does that make me feel better or worse? Who are they? How much did it cost them compared to what I have, and what exactly have they given up? Without all these questions being answered, their contribution does not mean anything to me; they live in a different world to the one I experience.

116. See www.gov.uk/government/statistics/rough-sleeping-snapshot-in-england-autumn-2020/rough-sleeping-snapshot-in-england-autumn-2020 (accessed 24 August 2021).
117. Rawls, *A Theory of Justice*, p. 14.

Loving our neighbour as ourselves involves interaction. Rawls' scheme makes no judgement about the significance of 'belonging' because the spiritual aspects of his theory are subsumed into the category of freedom of thought and conscience. Of course, I would make an agreement to insure that my basic needs are met if I don't know where I am going to end up behind that 'veil of ignorance'; but when I do find out where I am, what is it that will hold me to that previous agreement? I certainly won't want to keep it if other people start to ignore their original commitment, and even if that does not happen, might I fall to the temptation to get as much money as I could? The force of Christ's moral teaching was based on the tug-of-war between our selfish[118] and compassionate instincts, while Rawls' model of liberal democracy is built on an idealised view of human nature, as rational agents with no previous history.

Rawls' uses a hypothetical position of ignorance, innocence and reasoning to try to predict what a liberal democracy should be like. The Christian message is one of recognition of both the positive and negative sides of our nature, reconciliation and repair. We are made in the image of God[119] but we also fall short of that image. It follows for the Christian that loving our neighbour as ourselves is bound up with loving God, because God is the source of love, a love that involves sacrifice as well as affection. What has been given to us should not be held to ourselves alone; that was William Hartley's belief.

Q. What are the limits of democracy?

---

118. The Old Testament story of Naaman, an army commander being cured of leprosy by Elisha, a man of God from Israel, illustrates the human trait of dissatisfaction with what we have. After Naaman had been cured of his leprosy he offered various gifts to Elisha, who refused them. Elisha's servant Gehazi thought otherwise, caught Naaman up and told him a concocted story in order to be given gifts. When Elisha saw Gehazi again, Gehazi denied doing anything, but he himself was struck down with leprosy as a consequence of his deception. Even when a situation is dealt with peacefully with a good outcome, the desire for more than is our due can overtake us. See 2 Kings 5.

119. Genesis 1:26-27.

Chapter Five: Theocracy

Theocracy is a system of government which is seen as God-given; policy is not in the hands of the people. Rather, religious leaders who see themselves as God's representatives mould doctrines into laws which are then imposed onto the people. The relevant punishments are also decided upon by those leaders. They are the law makers and the law enforcers; there is no independent judiciary. In medieval times through to the Renaissance, the Papacy sought to act as a theocracy with varying levels of success, depending on how much support they received from monarchs and their armies. However, theocracy is still a form of government in the twenty-first century, particularly in the Middle East. In August 2021, the United States withdrew from Afghanistan; the Taliban took control and instituted an Islamic theocracy. There are five other Islamic nations which can be said to be theocracies as well as the Vatican City; they are Iran, Saudi Arabia, Mauritania, Sudan and Yemen. They either have religious leaders who exercise absolute political control or governments who implement religious law.[120]

Many Christians are sorry to be living in what is said to be a post-Christian culture, but what exactly would be involved in a modern Christian theocracy? What particular laws would be introduced that do not currently exist? How would a 'Christian' government treat the issue of the rights of non-believers or those from other faiths? Would the government take a view on sexuality or leave it as a matter of individual conscience? How would capital punishment be viewed? Crucially, would the government allow elections through which a non-Christian government might be elected?

---

120. In English medieval history there have been some very close alliances between the monarchy and the Church, but the head of the Church and the monarch were never one and the same person. Heretics were often identified by the Church and executed by the state.

If theocracy is to be sustained *over time*, free democratic elections have to be restricted, manipulated or abolished. Theocratic religious leaders might justify their position because they claim to have a mandate from God to do so. Releasing power to the people through an unimpeded electoral process would be a sign of disloyalty to the very doctrine that justifies that position in the first place. However, there would also be a loss of political power which might be interpreted as a signal of divine disapproval.

From a purely psychological perspective, the more power someone holds the more wary they become about the motives of others in unseating them. The sufferers of domestic violence and victims of child abuse report how threats to their loved ones are used as silencing devices. Those who rule by muscle have to adopt a Machiavellian approach; they have to use fear as a means of control.

Humility is a particular problem for theocratic leaders. Christ taught that 'the last will be first, and the first will be last'.[121] Would leaders give up their position because they knew they had done wrong, even if they had not been caught out? Would they lead by example and admit mistakes and turn back from unwise decisions? How does being 'poor in spirit', meek, pursuing righteousness, being merciful, 'pure in heart' and a peacemaker[122] fit into running a country? How dissimilar to secular politics would theocratic Christian politics be?

Q. Is there a place for humility in politics?

Every person is created in the image of God and so has inestimable worth. Consequently, if citizens do not follow the Christian faith they should not be treated *differently* by government as far as their human

121. Matthew 20:16.
122. See Matthew 5:3-10.

rights are concerned.[123] As God gave humankind choice, so governments should enable freedom of conscience in matters of faith. Even if every single person in a society was a convinced follower of Christ, it is more than likely that there would be sceptics and non-believers in the second and subsequent generations. A Christian theocracy is a contradiction in terms, because taking the step of faith in Christ should be a *free* choice; the imposition of faith is to remove its essence and replace it with outward observance, through coercive control.

Does this mean that Christians should advocate for a system of government that allows people sufficient freedom to practise and witness to their faith? Before Christ ascended to heaven, He said this to the disciples: 'Therefore go and make disciples of all nations, baptising them in the name of the Father and of the Son and of the Holy Spirit'.[124] He did *not* say 'Go and take over the governments of all nations and then compel all to be baptised in the name of the Father and of the Son and of the Holy Spirit'. If we want the freedom to witness and make disciples from every nation, it follows that we should want all nations to support such freedoms. It does not make sense to argue for a government that allows sufficient freedom for the exercise of the Christian faith but no other. To do that is to deny the existence of any real choice or any common respect.

Q. Why would a Christian theocratic government be more likely to be concerned with outward observance rather than inner renewal?

Democracy is a system which is open to competing influences. It follows that Christians are free to advocate for whatever laws they feel would be consistent with their faith and their moral outlook: if they are successfully adopted, they will be democratically approved rather than the result of autocratic dictates. The Christian aspiration is *not* to take

---

123. Please see Driscoll, *The Good Question*, pp, 50-52.

124 Matthew 28:19.

over the running of the system, but to ensure that the system is used to promote a fair and just society in which there is sufficient freedom to love God and love our neighbours as ourselves. 'Render to Caesar the things that are Caesar's, and to God the things that are God's.'[125] In saying that taxation was rightfully owed to Caesar, Christ also implied that the system to levy it was also Caesar's. He did not suggest that the synagogue should take over the collection and distribution of taxation.

I would advocate for laws that restrict trading with countries which breach human rights conventions, laws that prevent banks and financial institutions from investing in products which damage the environment and laws that limit arms sales to democratic nations solely for their own military forces. These will not be the priorities that other Christians might make, and that in itself shows the need for government to find a balance between social order and political freedom.

Justifying theocracy

Theocracy, as I have already said, is where religious leaders claim to interpret divine teaching and apply it to the citizens of the state they rule over. Judaism, Christianity and Islam have all had periods when theocracy was held as a divinely sanctioned form of government. For the Jews in exile in ancient Egypt, the Promised Land was there to be reached, provided they were obedient to God.[126] For Christians responding to the expansion of the Islamic empire in the latter part of the first millennium, political and territorial control of the Holy Land

---

125. Mark 12:17, KJV.

126. Leviticus 20:22-24: Keep all my decrees and laws and follow them, so that the land where I am bringing you to live may not vomit you out. You must not live according to the customs of the nations I am going to drive out before you. Because they did all these things, I abhorred them. But I said to you, "You will possess their land; I will give it to you as an inheritance, a land flowing with milk and honey." I am the LORD your God, who has set you apart from the nations.'

would be a sign of God's approval.[127] For Muslims the formation of an Islamic state was a stated ambition from the very beginning when Mohammed was alive.[128]

Theocratic government is closely connected to how freedom of conscience is viewed. Is that freedom a blessing or a curse? Suppressing independence of mind can be justified through the idea that otherwise it leads to selfish, destructive and divinely forbidden behaviour. If governments suppress the use of freedom *itself* on that basis, that suppression can be justified as pleasing to God regardless of the means. The contrary idea of leaving spiritual repair and development to the mercy of free choice is anathema to those who see human nature as a mix of passions which can *only* be restrained by coercive control.

If inner change is the key to spiritual development, then political systems which encourage free thinking in the democratic tradition will be essential; this is based on the belief that human beings can only genuinely change for the better if they are not held under a psychological

---

127. Please see the section 'Holy orders to kill' in Chapter One.

128. One key difference between the histories of early Christian and Islamic believers is Pentecost. In Christianity the coming of the Holy Spirit gave the disciples the energy and courage to go out into the world and preach the good news of Christ's suffering and resurrection, a victory through His identification with death and the destructive intent of human beings which was overturned on the third day.

In Islam the Prophet himself, although preaching peace and acceptance of other faiths, led a military action to defend an attack on Medina in 625 where his followers lived. Karen Armstrong, who says the action should not be judged by standards of our own time, writes: 'Muhammed showed no mercy. The seven hundred men of Qurayzah were killed, and their women and children sold as slaves.' Karen Armstrong, *Islam: A Short History* (London: Phoenix, 2000), p. 18. The Qurayzah were a Jewish tribe who sided with Mohammed's opponents in Mecca.

In early Islamic history in the two years following the death of the Prophet Mohammed, Abū Bakr suppressed those known as 'rejectionists' and 'apostates who opposed the early Muslim state'. Professor Hugh Kennedy says that the current Islamic State group derives inspiration from this. Hugh Kennedy, *The Caliphate* (London: Pelican, Penguin Random House, 2016), p. 374.

threat. That is not to say that society can maintain order without a system of criminal law, run by an independent judiciary: it is to say that the whole of the moral and political order should not be founded on the theory of divine threat, mediated by fallible human beings.

Is the law a divine blunt instrument based on suppression which can be justified as pleasing to God regardless of the level of distress and suffering caused along the way? Or is the law a way of enhancing the dignity of individuals through the concept of 'fairness'?

Here an independent judiciary is set up to discover the truth of the circumstance, and if a crime has been committed the punishment should take the level of intent into account. The individual's inviolable rights reappear.

Sharia Law is a form of law that is practised in full in some Islamic countries, partially in others and not at all in others who adopt secular legal systems.[129] Whereas Sharia law is infamous for such brutal punishments as amputation, stoning and flogging for acts of adultery, homosexuality or apostasy, there are many Islamic countries that do not go to such extremes and some like Malaysia who seek to integrate both civil and Sharia legal systems.[130]

The idea that leaders can mete out punishments because they have been told by God to act on His behalf assumes that the leaders have privileged access to God's intentions, and that they are able to carry out

---

129 https://worldpopulationreview.com/country-rankings/sharia-law-countries (accessed 2 September 2021).
See also Ashlea Hellman, 'The Convergence of International Human Rights and Sharia Law. Can International Ideals and Muslim Religious Law Coexist?', 2016, https://nysba.org/NYSBA/Sections/International/Awards/2016%20Pergam%20Writing%20Competition/submissions/Hellmann%20Ashlea.pdf (accessed 2 September 2021).
130. Victoria Soh, 'A Tale of Two Systems', 9 December 2020, www.durhamasian-lawjournal.com/post/a-tale-of-two-systems-sharia-and-civil-law-in-malaysia (accessed 2 September 2021).

them out precisely as instructed. From a Christian perspective, both of these assumptions are false; when God spoke to Moses as he was nearing the end of his life, he was told that the Israelites would worship false gods and indulge in corrupt practices. But in the song which Moses sang to the people, God said, 'It is mine to avenge; I will repay.'[131] St Paul, in confirming that we are not divine henchmen, quoted that same verse in his letter to the Romans:

> Do not repay anyone evil for evil. Be careful to do what is right in the eyes of everyone. If it is possible, as far as it depends on you, live at peace with everyone. Do not take revenge, my dear friends, but leave room for God's wrath, for it is written: 'It is mine to avenge; I will repay,' says the Lord. On the contrary: 'If your enemy is hungry, feed him; if he is thirsty, give him something to drink. In doing this, you will heap burning coals on his head.' Do not be overcome by evil, but overcome evil with good.[132]

The lesson is clear; we are not agents of divine wrath, but by doing good in the face of wrongdoing, a genuine change of heart can take place. This is what is meant by 'heaping burning coals on someone's head'. 'If your enemy is hungry, feed him …'

The end of politics

The idea that human beings are essentially corruptible unless controlled is essential to the theocratic mindset. The theory is that when we are controlled by religious leaders there will be no need for political debate.

---

131. Deuteronomy 32:35.
132. Romans 12:17-21.

Such absolute authority rules out any effective representations to those in power.

There is an equally powerful voice written by a European Enlightenment writer which promotes the case for absolute authority. Thomas Hobbes, already referred to in Chapter Three, believed that our core fears were based on the insecurity we feel about being taken advantage of by other people. Without a system of control, we are at the mercy of unscrupulous others who will, without hesitation, steal our property, ravage our families and leave us destitute. We prefer to take the risk of being mistreated by an authority than by a neighbour who might do the same again and again. For Hobbes, the state of our nature means we must owe absolute allegiance to the Sovereign in power, regardless of their character, and that Sovereign must reign absolutely.

Thomas Hobbes' analysis of human nature appears to be extreme in our Western democracies, but many caught in the crossfire between theocratic rule and tribal conflict are faced with a choice between absolute authority and chaos. As already mentioned, in August 2021, the United States withdrew their forces from Afghanistan after twenty years of working with Afghans in an attempt to build a national Western-styled government strong enough to resist the pressures from the Taliban, previously known to provide refuge for terrorists. The periodical *The Economist* said this:

> … a purely military approach to fighting jihadism does little to make the ground less fertile for it … If the old Afghan government had been less corrupt and less inept at dealing with tribal power brokers, it might have proved more resilient … Unless existing states provide basic services and something resembling justice, the jihadists' siren will always sound seductive.[133]

133. 'After Afghanistan, where next for global jihad?' *The Economist*, 28 August-3 September 2021, p. 9.

94

Any authority is better than no authority at all, or so some might think if we were in that position. Living under a theocratic or totalitarian regime presents dilemmas that living under a democracy does not. For the many hungry and malnourished children in Afghanistan today, neither option means anything.[134] Under such circumstances, the right to participate in politics is a far-flung hope.

There are two further theories which include the idea that there will be an end to politics. Plato's (427-347 BC) republic was built on the notion that everyone, including women and slaves, would be content with their lot; they would be content for the male philosopher elite to debate and then issue edicts. It was a hierarchical society with no need for complaints procedures or customer feedback mechanisms.

Karl Marx (1818-83), on the other hand, envisioned a progressive history which would, after the turmoil of revolution, reveal a state of harmony where no government would be needed as all would be in agreement as to how society should be run. Marx's case was that once unfairness concerning material resources was eradicated, there would be no other controversial issues.

Plato's absolute authority of philosopher males is equivalent to theocratic rule, but without the divine element. Marx's idea of a collective will also excludes any substantive role for religious influence. Both Marx and Plato assume that human beings can reach some kind of quiet tranquillity under the right conditions; both theories are unrealised and are based on an idealised view of human nature.

Theocracy, on the other hand, does not make that move, preferring to confer on religious elites the task of controlling the wilder passions which are part of the human condition. Totalitarian regimes and full-blown

---

134. Christina Wilkie, '1 million Afghan children are at risk of starvation, UNICEF director warns', 14 September 2021, CNBC. See www.cnbc.com/2021/09/13/1-million-afghan-children-at-risk-of-starvation-unicef-chief-warns-.html (accessed 6 November 2021).

theocracies are essentially repressive and take pride in being so, even if their press briefings are designed to convince the listeners otherwise.

Human nature

Marx's end state was similar in conception to philosopher Jean-Jacques Rousseau's description of human beings as we originally were; that is, a state where harmony would prevail unless an external threat presented itself. Rousseau (1712-78) thought that humans were originally docile, without language and living like the higher social animals. Hobbes and Locke also had their own versions of how people were in the original state of nature. All these political philosophers used the idea of origins to explain how human development threw up the need for government; as civilisation, agriculture and dominance over our environment grew, a structure to regulate society was required.

Fundamental to the modern idea of creating a system of government was the notion of an agreement or contract between the people and the rulers. For Locke, that agreement was conditional on the rulers carrying out their 'job specification', preserving liberty and property. For Hobbes, it was an unconditional acceptance of any form of government because the alternative of anarchy was untenable. For Rousseau, the will of the people would form a type of 'self-government' which would take on a life of its own should any individual challenge it, and challenge it to their cost.

The problem with the formation of these contracts or agreements is that they are hypothetical; the reality is that everyone is born into a set of prior arrangements. By the time we are developed sufficiently to 'recognise the selfhood of others' we are already *in* a society.[135] We are born into families with no prior agreements as to how we will be treated.

---

135. Roger Scruton, *A Short History of Modern Philosophy* (London: Routledge, 1995; second edn), p. 204.

We are not there in advance to make decisions with others about what kind of government we will have in society once it gets going. It is only as we become aware of the scope of our freedoms that we are able to then form agreements, make representations and engage in politics, if the institutions of our society allow so.

The Christian conception of original sin parallels this reasoning; before we are born we are not asked if we want to trust God or not. We arrive in this world with no sense of being connected to God; that we live in a broken world – and one with fractured relationships presents itself to most of us soon enough. If we are to start the journey of faith, it is from a predetermined place.

The doctrine of original sin tells us that we are not starting from a neutral position when it comes to repairing our relationship with God. What modern political philosophers tell us is that the political institutions of society are constructed by *us*. It follows that our institutions are as fallible as we are. Theocracy is a form of government that uses fallible men, more often than not, to control our fallible natures, but spiritual rebirth for the Christian is about inner realisation, not political control.

Q. Why do you think Christ said 'the last will be first, and the first will be last'?[136]

---

136. Matthew 20:16.

Conclusion

The politics of God's wrath or reconciliation

The difference between standing up for the poor and the vulnerable and exacting punishments *on behalf of* God is a crucial one. When we read that God used evil people to punish the children of Israel, we might be tempted to say, 'If God can do that why can't we?'[137] Can I hire someone to kill the drug dealer who is selling drugs to my child? What is wrong with damaging the owner of substandard properties who is charging very high rents? Can I arrange for people who I believe are behaving in some sort of immoral way to be harassed? Should politicians adopt the same tactics?

'A good tree cannot bear bad fruit, and a bad tree cannot bear good fruit.'[138] Christ insisted that our outer attitudes and actions should reflect our inner lives. For Christ, the means do not justify the ends because God's character is not duplicitous or manipulative. Our light should shine so that others might 'see [our] good deeds and glorify [our] Father in heaven'.[139] We are made to be pure in heart, even though we never fully are.

We expect governments to formulate policies, we expect professionals to implement those policies, but how can they stand any chance of fruition if there is no partnership from the community at large? We cannot resolve drug dealing without effective policing, both at home and abroad, education, and protection for young people and proper mentoring for those at risk. These measures are, of course, examples of the issues politicians and civil servants deal with on our behalf. Often

---

137. See 2 Kings 21:12.
138. Matthew 7:18.
139. Matthew 5:16.

the practicalities, including recruiting and training skilled staff, are more complex than creating the appropriate legislation. It is far easier to say what should be done than working out the best way to actually do it.

In a society where people increasingly work, live and spend leisure time with different sets of people, the force of communal togetherness is under increasing pressure. To use the example already given, there are areas where drug dealing and criminality need restraining before any effective community building can take place. Reconciliation does not mean that restraint and appropriate punishments are not required, but it does mean that in themselves they are insufficient.

Enacting God's justice is not about trying to second guess if He wants us to act as if we were Him. Once we recognise that God's prime purpose is to reconcile rather than punish, the confusion as to which comes first is resolved. As much as we need proper legal restraints with appropriate punishments, we know that that inner change does not occur through punishment. If the Old Testament story of the children of Israel proves anything, it proves that. Punishments do not change hearts, even if they might teach restraint; sometimes they stop bad behaviour and sometimes they protect society from dangerous people. However, knowing that I might get caught does not make me change the *inclination* I might have to harm others either for my own gain or for the feeling of power it might provide. In Chapter Three I recounted an argument I witnessed at a local café. The police could only do so much, but the spiritual and moral implications were left unattended.

Politics is not a hobby; immense experience and wisdom is needed to know when and by what means to counteract deprivation, abuse and exploitation. Some problems are beyond immediate repair, such as the Israeli-Palestinian question; others conceal resentments behind an uneasy peace, such as in Northern Ireland. Some problems are undermined by international criminality, such as the importing of hard drugs, and some are increased by the facilitation of investment from anywhere on the globe into fossil fuels, more and more deadly weapons, or surveillance systems for totalitarian regimes.

Compromises, stalemates, bargaining and group loyalties all play into the equations that politicians are asked to solve. How difficult is it to hold on to the principle of reconciliation in the midst of all this? That challenge is not a challenge for the politician alone, it is for all. A policy designed to end a long-running conflict cannot succeed without a community which is also looking in the same direction. If politicians do not set standards of honesty and integrity then executives, police forces, media outlets and businesses are hardly likely to follow suit. Where does that leave everyone else?

What does the Christian account of reconciliation really mean? The skill of a politician, a manager or anyone in authority is in both their expertise and their character. When we look at the life of Christ, we see that He reacted differently according to whatever situation He was in, but it is impossible, for me at least, to find any sense of Him being duplicitous, manipulative or self-seeking. Perhaps that is the key: a deep knowledge of the human condition and an equally deep motivation to bring about reconciliation.

The parable of the tenants was a story of a landowner who sent servant after servant to collect the fruit of the vineyard; each one was killed by the tenants and eventually the landowner sent his son who was also killed by them.[140] The picture Christ was drawing is that the servants were those who spoke for God in the Old Testament and that He Himself was the son of the landowner. So God Himself became a human being, and a new order of inner repair was instigated through Christ's suffering and the overcoming of death with which we are so familiar. True reconciliation is a deeply costly business.

---

140. Matthew 21:33-42.

Political culture

How can we gauge the extent to which religious belief is incorporated into national identity?[141] At the softer end, a majority in a nation affiliate themselves with a particular faith but the formal links with the state are not strong enough to dictate major policy changes; the United Kingdom in the twentieth century onwards is an example. There are some formal links between the government and the monarchy, which is itself head of the Church of England, but the Church does not in any sense determine the direction of overall economic and foreign policy, even if it might take a special interest in issues such as religious education.

Religious influence is much more significant when the law enshrines differential treatment for certain minorities. Before homosexuality was decriminalised in 1967, a significant religious lobby was in support of maintaining the status quo. A historic example of religious discrimination was under Caliph Umar 11 (717-720) when non-Muslims were made to pay a land tax.[142] A current example is in Iran where Christians, Jews and Zoroastrians are restricted under the law as to how freely they can practise their faith; the Bahá'i, the fourth religious minority, have no legal rights at all. Sunni Muslims also are discriminated against in respect of employment opportunities.[143]

Buddhism is the majority religion in Myanmar and its scriptures decry violence. Since 2012, Rohingya Muslims who originally came into

---

141. The following typology is adapted from and summarised in Milan Vaishnav, ed., *The BJP in Power: Indian Democracy and Religious Nationalism*, Chapter 1 by Milan Vaishnav, pp. 8-9, Carnegie Endowment for International Peace, https://carnegieendowment.org/files/BJP_In_Power_final.pdf (accessed 9 September 2021).

142. See Kennedy, *The Caliphate*, p. 75.

143. 'Discrimination against religious minorities in IRAN Report presented by the FIDH (Fédération Internationale des Ligues des Droits de L'homme) and the Ligue de Défense des Droits de l'Homme en Iran 63rd session of the Committee on the Elimination of Racial Discrimination August 2003' www.fidh.org/IMG/pdf/ir0108a.pdf (accessed 20 September 2021).

Myanmar from neighbouring Bangladesh have been persecuted by the military and also by many Buddhists.

> In December 2017, Doctors Without Borders estimated that over 10,000 Rohingya had been killed in the most recent upsurge of violence, and that about 700,000 are living in exile in neighboring Bangladesh and India, causing the UN Human Rights chief to state the situation was 'a textbook example of ethnic cleansing.'[144]

The boundary between genocide and ethnic cleansing is blurred. When religious identity is used to vilify the character of outsiders, it becomes a vehicle which can be used by unscrupulous political and military leaders to maintain control. Geographical boundaries come to symbolise the religious differences and so expelling the 'outsider' becomes a quasi-religious activity. Nationalism and religious imperialism are very closely bound up in such situations.

The most extreme position, the type of theocracy I described in the previous chapter, is where political and legal rule are reinforced by 'divine' edict, against which there is little or no appeal. Even though there are religious minorities in Iran, as already mentioned, the overall political structure is defined in the following way:

> The peculiarity of the Islamic Republic of Iran is not the mere fact that Islam is the religion of the State (other States share the same feature) but rather the fact that the State itself is conceived as an institution and instrument of the divine will. In this system,

---

144. Randy Rosenthal, 'What's the Connection between Buddhism and Ethnic Cleansing in Myanmar?' Lions Roar: Buddhist Wisdom for Our Time, 13 November 2018. See www.lionsroar.com/what-does-buddhism-have-to-do-with-the-ethnic-cleansing-in-myanmar/ (accessed 4 October 2021).

which can best be described as a clerical oligarchy, there is an identification between divine truth and clerical authority.[145]

One critical quality of any system which purports to represent Christian values is that *every* person should be treated with dignity and impartiality under the law. When you read the Sermon on the Mount, you often hear Christ say, 'You have heard that it was said ... But I tell you ...'[146] Using this form of words, Christ first quoted a part of the law and then added a point as to how it could be expanded, more often than not referring to our deeper instincts. And who was He talking about: our enemies, our brothers, those who take us to court, effectively everyone.[147]

Christianity is a faith of heart and mind and for the Church to express itself without intimidation or threat, the social order has to incorporate a measure of political freedom. Democratic freedom is not the end goal for the Christian, as Donald Carson says, because God wants us to use the freedom we have to serve God and experience His grace.[148] Freedom

---

145. 'Discrimination against religious minorities in IRAN Report presented by the FIDH(Fédération Internationale des Ligues des Droits de L'homme) and the Ligue de Défense des Droits de l'Homme en Iran 63rd session of the Committee on the Elimination of Racial Discrimination August 2003' www.fidh.org/IMG/pdf/ir0108a.pdf (accessed on 20 September 2021), p. 5.

146. For example, Matthew 5:21-22.

147. There is sometimes a debate about a 'choice' between doing something socially worthwhile or witnessing about Christ's work of salvation. After many years in social work, working with people from many other faiths and with no faith, I have found that doing something worthwhile with others has its own value. One reason why I haven't automatically told other people that I am doing it because I am a Christian is because that is not true. I would have done it anyway because I recognise it as something valuable in itself. Hence I could collaborate with anyone who genuinely wanted to make a positive difference to other people's lives. The fact that I am a Christian has come out naturally in the normal course of relationships rather than as a justification for social action, which self-evidently needs doing.

148. Donald A. Carson, *Christ & Culture Revisited* (Grand Rapids, MI: William B. Eerdmans Publishing, 2008), pp. 138-139.

can just as easily be used to destroy as it can to enhance; it is a gift to be used for a purpose. Therefore, Christians have an obligation to work out fair and impartial political arrangements *with* all and *for* all; the alternative is to discriminate and even oppress religious minorities. If we do not want such things done to us, how can we possibly contemplate doing the same to others?[149]

Truth or lies

We live in a society where different ideas about truth live alongside one another.[150] We are perhaps unsure whether truth is about the way the natural world works or the way people relate to each other. Every generation seems to want throw off some of the old ways and in a media saturated existence we are overloaded with images, peer influences and many forms of entertainment. In this context to talk about truth is almost old fashioned. Our culture seems more certain as to what freedom means. However, when it comes to politics tussling over *who*, if anyone, is telling the truth, matters.

---

149. Christian theologian Richard H. Niebuhr's wrote about the degree to which Christians should dip their toe into the water of the culture they find themselves in. His models started from a theological viewpoint; what does God think about the extent we should become involved in the culture we find ourselves in? His models range from a complete separation between spiritual and earthly life to almost complete accommodation. Within this range is the idea of Christians transforming society's values, institutions and priorities. The options are not prescriptive or mutually exclusive; they are intended to enhance understanding and aides to help Christians assess each particular context. Please see Timothy Keller, *Center Church* (Grand Rapids, MI: Zondervan, 2012), p. 194

150. Basil Mitchell, *Law, Morality and Religion in a Secular Society* (Oxford: Oxford University Press, 1967), p. 98. Basil Mitchell describes three approaches, all of which connect up the idea of truth with freedom. The first says that our freedom is derived from beliefs about our intended purpose; for Christians that means our freedom is there to glorify God. The second type is the freedom that can only be worked out by us; we *alone* discover the truth about ourselves and the kind of society that suits us best. The third type is freedom that leads to nowhere but back to its starting point; there is no end point or truth to be discovered.

That there is a truth to tell rather than a smoke screen to be puffed out is never far from the surface of day-to-day political life. Bending the truth to suit our own purposes is not the same as presenting a case clearly. What is the difference? Hiding errors and exaggerating successes, using statistics selectively to give a false picture, writing histories which point away from our own mistakes; these are the devices which mislead. Talking about mistakes as well as successes, taking responsibility rather than blaming others, admitting uncertainty as opposed to predicting a better life for all; these are the means through which honesty can be reinstated.

William Wilberforce (1759-1833) took a leading role in the campaign to abolish slavery during the twenty years from 1787 to 1807. It is clear that his Christian faith was instrumental in his own conviction that slavery was wrong.[151] What is less well known is that in the seventeenth and early eighteenth centuries 'Protestant slave owners in the English, Dutch and Danish colonies tended to view conversion as inconsistent or incompatible with slavery'.[152] For more than 100 years from 1670 onwards, Protestant missionaries were in conflict with slave owners as to whether slaves would be more loyal and hardworking if they converted to Christianity and were baptised. We have much to celebrate in terms of the part Christians played in outlawing slavery, but also much to lament in the part we played in perpetuating it. We should tell the *whole* truth, even when it is uncomfortable.

It is not usually considered politically astute to admit wrong or error, unless it is uncovered. The Pharisees said this to Christ:

---

151. See:
www.bbc.co.uk/religion/religions/christianity/people/williamwilberforce_1.shtml (accessed 21 September 2021).

152. See Katharine Gerbner, *Christian Slavery: Conversion and Race in the Protestant Atlantic World*, (Philadelphia, PA: University of Pennsylvania Press, 2018), pp. 2-4.

'Teacher,' they said, 'we know that you are a man of integrity and that you teach the way of God in accordance with the truth. You aren't swayed by others, because you pay no attention to who they are. Tell us then, what is your opinion? Is it right to pay the poll-tax to Caesar or not?' But Jesus, knowing their evil intent, said, 'You hypocrites, why are you trying to trap me? Show me the coin used for paying the tax.' They brought him a denarius, and he asked them, 'Whose image is this? And whose inscription?' 'Caesar's,' they replied. Then he said to them, 'So give back to Caesar what is Caesar's, and to God what is God's.' When they heard this, they were amazed. So they left him and went away.[153]

Many pages have been written about Christ's answer, and I have added a few, but His insight into the motivation behind the question was as equally telling as His answer to their question. The truth of the questions we ask and the things we say to justify our position are as much about our inner intentions as they are about the issues themselves. For politicians, this is a key point: if I am a politician, am I pointing out wrongdoing or am I seeking to gain personal advantage? Am I seeking to manipulate the system while appearing to be interested in the good of others? Or am I prepared to stand up for honesty and fairness, even if doing so affects my personal position?

The heart of the matter

Christ was insistent that the root of change is spiritual. He was also clear that seeking power and status in itself was ultimately fruitless. What He constantly made clear beyond doubt was that simply signing up to the religious status quo and carrying out the expected rituals did not cut any ice with God. And so a Christian culture, if such a thing exists, cannot

153. Matthew 22:16-22.

be about a majority of people affirming the creed or taking over political institutions. It has to be about the character rather than the name of God. It has to be less worried about calling something Christian than actually being it. What, then, is 'being it'? How can I try to summarise it?

The prophets described God as truthful, holy, compassionate and angry when God was disobeyed. Christ described the Father as the source of goodness, above the meanderings of earthly power struggles and unequivocal about the connection between motivation and honesty; to want something but deceive in order to get it is to disregard others. Christ put it like this: 'God is spirit, and his worshippers must worship in the Spirit and in truth.'[154] We have already seen that God is not content to 'deprive the poor of their rights and withhold justice … '[155] If we see what God's love can mean for ourselves, then we can also see what it means for other people.

Where we find compassion we find the imprint of God's character. Where we find challenges to injustice which resist corruption, the abuse of human rights and the neglect of the poor and marginalised we find a resonance with the sayings of the prophets and of Christ Himself. When we put our own hands to the plough, whether as rulers or citizens, counting the interests of others higher than our own, we are genuinely bringing what Christ stands for into our culture. That doesn't mean we will solve the problem or be recognised as doing something valuable. Nevertheless, when we bring a sense of integrity to whatever role we have, whatever Christ has done for us personally will come out; there will be no need to contrive it, no need to say, 'By the way, I did that because I am a Christian.'

154. John 4:24.
155. Isaiah 10:2.

Conclusion

And when you pray, do not be like the hypocrites, for they love to pray standing in the synagogues and on the street corners to be seen by others. Truly I tell you, they have received their reward in full. But when you pray, go into your room, close the door and pray to your Father, who is unseen. Then your Father, who sees what is done in secret, will reward you.[156]

---

156. Matthew 6:5-6.

References

Karen Armstrong, *Islam: A Short History* (London: Phoenix, 2000).

St Augustine, *City of God* (trans. Henry Bettenson, 1972; London: Penguin Classics, 2003, first published 1467).

Frederick Fyvie Bruce, *The New Testament Documents: Are They Reliable?* (San Francisco, CA: Bottom of the Hill Publishing, 2013).

Andrew Bunt, *People Not Pronouns, Reflections on Transgender Experience* (Cambridge: Grove Books, 2021).

Marigold Best and Pamela Hussey, *A Culture of Peace, Women, Faith and Reconciliation* (London: Catholic Institute for International Relations, 2005).

Jacques-Bénigne Bossuet, Patrick Riley, ed., *Politics Drawn From Holy Scripture*, Cambridge Texts in the History of Political Thought (Cambridge: Cambridge University Press, 1990).

Donald A. Carson, *Christ & Culture Revisited* (Grand Rapids, MI: William B. Eerdmans Publishing, 2008).

Carlos R. Colindres, *El Salvador Today* (Great Britain: Amazon, 2020).

Patrick Devlin, *The Enforcement of Morals* (Oxford: Oxford University Press, 1965).

Nathan Driscoll, *The God Dilemma: A Philosophical Walk for the Undecided* (Welwyn Garden City: Malcolm Down, 2020).

Nathan Driscoll, *The Good Question* (Welwyn Garden City: Malcolm Down, 2021).

Ronald Dworkin, *Taking Right Seriously*, (London: Duckworth, 1977).

Peter Frankopan, *The New Silk Roads: The Present and Future of the World* (London: Bloomsbury Publishing, 2019).

Dan Jones, *The Templars: The Rise and Fall of God's Holy Warriors* (London: Head of Zeus, 2017).

Bamber Gascoigne, *A Brief History of Christianity* (London: Robinson, 2003).

Katharine Gerbner, *Christian Slavery: Conversion and Race in the Protestant Atlantic World*, (Philadelphia, PA: University of Pennsylvania Press, 2018).

Tom Holland, *Dominion: The Making of the Western Mind*, (London: Little, Brown Book Group, 2019).

Timothy Keller, *Generous Justice* (London: Hodder & Stoughton, 2010).

Hugh Kennedy, *The Caliphate* (London: Pelican, Penguin Random House, 2016).

Gordon & Stephen Kuhrt, *Believing in Baptism: Understanding and Living God's Covenant Sign* (London: T&T Clark, 2020).

John Locke, *The First and Second Treatises of Government* (originally published anonymously in 1689, reprinted in Great Britain by Amazon).

Basil Mitchell, *Law, Morality and Religion in a Secular Society* (Oxford: Oxford University Press, 1967).

John Rawls, *A Theory of Justice* (Oxford: Oxford University Press, 1971).

Alan Ryan, *On Politics: A History of Political Thought From Heredotus to the Present* (London: Liveright Publishing Corporation, 2012).

Alec Ryrie, *Protestants: The Radicals Who Made the Modern World* (London: William Collins, 2017).

Roger Scruton, *A Short History of Modern Philosophy* (London: Routledge, 1995; second edn).